UNDER THREE TSARS

UNDER THREE TSARS

THE MEMOIRS OF THE LADY-IN-WAITING

ELIZABETH NARISHKIN-KURAKIN

Edited by

RENÉ FÜLÖP-MILLER

Translated from the German by

JULIA E. LOESSER

E. K. Naryshkina

WITH FIFTY ILLUSTRATIONS

NEW YORK

E. P. DUTTON & CO., INC.

FIRST EDITION

PREFACE

THE BOLSHEVISTS look upon the days before 1917 as a sort of prehistoric period to the "new communistic humanity." They regard the representatives of the past as we look upon the people and the culture of the Stone Age.

When one visits the palaces of the former lords of Russia, the rooms, articles of luxury and utensils of which are arranged museographically and displayed to the pupils of the Communist schools as relics of a barbaric or pre-communistic epoch, it would seem indeed that in Russia a whole species of mankind had been extirpated to its last representative.

These people do, as a matter of fact, live in concealment. One may see them clothed in shabby garments in the midst of noisy vendors at the great fairs; the ladies sew in competition with the girls of the Proletariat; the once-proud gentlemen are reduced to doing chores as laborers, shoeblacks, cleaners or cloakroom attendants.

During my last visit to Russia, an accident gave me the opportunity of entering into this buried world of pre-Revolutionary society. But more valuable than all other reports were the memoirs of that venerable lady who had occupied the highest posts of honor in those days of bygone splendor. When Elizabeth Narishkin-Kurakin opened her yellowing diaries and read to me, when she told of Madame Récamier and Chateaubriand whom she had seen as a child, or of Napoleon III, and Eugenie, whose guest she had been, or of the great Chancellor Gortshakow or of Dostoyevski, who frequented her Salon, of Alexander II, his tragic love affair, and his still more tragic end, of Alexander III and his Councilor, Pobyedonostzev, or of Nicholas II, and his Alice with all of whom Elizabeth Narishkin lived on terms of intimate friendship,—then the history of nearly a century rises from her descriptions which begins with the French Revolution and ends with the Russian Upheaval.

In kind compliance to my entreaties, Elizabeth Narishkin consented to arrange her notes and to write down for posterity to read, all that she had recounted to me on many an evening in her poor little room in Moscow.

These are her memoirs which I am now offering to the public.

She finally succeeded in fleeing from Russia to Paris, where she died recently in the Russian Emigrants' Home, Sainte Geneviève des Bois. With her death, one of the most fascinating personalities of Old Russia has gone forever.

RENÉ FÜLÖP-MILLER.

Vienna, April 29, 1930.

LIST OF ILLUSTRATIONS

NOTE

In this book the proper names have been spelled to approximate as nearly as possible their Russian pronunciation.

THE TRANSLATOR.

UNDER THREE TSARS

UNDER THREE TSARS

CHAPTER I

Sojourn of My Parents in Vienna and Paris—First Impressions of Childhood—The Countess de Valence—Her Memories of the French Revolution—A Children's Ball at Madame Récamier's and Chateaubriand—The Princess Bagration—A Journey From Paris to St. Petersburg in the Forties—The Countess Apponyi—Arrival in St. Petersburg—Tatyana Potyemkin, the Friend of Two Tsars—Journey by Carriage to Moscow—Arrival at My Grandfather's—The Strange Etiquette in the Castle Kurakino—"Le Roi Boit"—"The Temple of Philosophy"—Serf-Orchestra and Serf-Theatre—A Court of State in Miniature—A Russian Prince Travels.

MY EARLIEST memories take me to Paris where my father, Prince Alexis Kurakin, was assigned Legation Counsellor to the Russian Embassy. The name of our family has been well known in the world of diplomacy for generations. In his memoirs, Saint Simon had already mentioned a Prince Boris Kurakin who under Louis XIV had been an Ambassador of Peter the Great in Paris.

I was one of three children, my parents being particularly attached to the oldest, Boris. He had been born soon after the death of their first child, and my parents saw in him God's own heavenly solace for that loss.

My father's diplomatic career had brought him first to Vienna, where later both my sister Alexandrine and my brother Fyodor were born. This sojourn in the Austrian capital had remained as particularly beautiful in their memory, and constituted a sunny chapter in the lives of my parents. My mother was then barely twenty-five years old and her charm and natural, graceful frankness won her promptly many friendships in Viennese society. As the Ambassador happened to be unmarried, my mother represented the hostess on all occasions, instead of the non-existent Ambassadress. From the reminiscences of my parents, I know that at that time they were in particular intimately associated with the Vicomte D'Arlincourt and with Marshal Marmont, Prince of Ragusa. As a born Princess Galitzine, my mother had, as a matter of course, admission to the most distinguished society.

In 1842, my father was transferred to Paris as First Secretary of the Embassy. I can still vividly see myself and our apartment there in the rue de Berris not far from the Russian Chapel. Above us lived the Countess de Valence, daughter of Madame de Genlis, a charming old lady whom my mother loved to visit. We children played often and with great pleasure with the grandchildren of the Countess, Bertrand de Caumont, and Mathilde and Geneviève de Loigle. On such occasions, we often listened to the old lady talk about her interesting memories and hearkened avidly, when she told of her imprisonment in the Conciergerie. At the time of the Great Revolution she had already been married, and it was her fate to see all the people who were dear to her ascend the scaffold. She herself only escaped execution through the timely overthrow of Robespierre.

During our visits to the Countess, almost regularly a queer intermezzo took place. From without, one would hear the crash of breaking china, whereupon Madame de Valence would call out to her servant: "Jacques, you have broken something again." And each time, the old man would answer, full of dignity and with a quaking voice: "Madame la Comtesse, one who does not handle things, never breaks anything."

At that time, I was invited to a children's ball at Madame Récamier's which was to take place in l'Abbaye au Bois. Throughout the entire forenoon of that gala day, the hairdresser worked over me with curl papers and curling irons; then he pressed a wreath of dewy primroses into my hair. I wore a white dress trimmed with Valenciennes lace and was as proud as a queen when an open carriage drove me to l'Abbaye au Bois. Upon my arrival, I was introduced to an old lady and to an old gentleman, and was told later that they were the famous Récamier and the no less famous M. de Chateaubriand.

At New Year's and at Easter time, we called regularly on an aunt of my mother's, the Princess Bagration, who lived in a charming house in the Rue St. Honoré, close to the Champs Elysées. She had been a famous beauty in her youth, and bore unmistakable traces of it, even as an old woman. Her features were of indescribable fineness, her skin as white as marble; she wore her hair in long blond curls and painstakingly removed every white hair. Always robed in delicate, diaphanous white fabrics, over pink or pale-blue undergarments, she reclined almost constantly on a couch which she left only to take drives in her well-known yellow landau. We children thought of this unusual woman, who was so different from other old ladies, as a sort of fairy, and were delighted when we were allowed to play in her garden.

Another important part in our lives was played by Madame Narishkin, a born Princess Lobanov-Rostovski, who had been an intimate friend of my grandmother, and who spoiled us as if we were her own grandchildren. Very dimly, I recall the famous Princess Lieven, who entertained lively social connections with my parents. I saw her at the festivities arranged for the Emperor. It was in the Russian Chapel whither she arrived dressed in a great bonnet, at the end of the Mass, as if to indicate that she was doing the Tsar a special honor.

In the spring of 1845, my parents decided to take a trip to Russia, as they had not seen their country for five years. Besides, my grandfather desired our visit. But as my father's affairs demanded all his attention, my mother took it upon herself to travel ahead to St. Petersburg with us children.

In those days, a journey of that kind meant adventure and hardships. The train ran only from Paris to Rouen, where we had to take a steamer which carried us on the Seine to Le Havre. Two steamers, the *Amsterdam* and the *Toge,* carried on the regular traffic between Le Havre and Kronstadt, and we had reserved passage on the *Amsterdam.* A friend of my mother, the Countess Apponyi, a former Countess Benkendorff, and her little boy, joined our party.

The last we saw of the land was our father waving good-bye to us; then the steamer hove out into the open sea and disappeared into the greenish-yellow waters of the North Sea.

Soon seasickness compelled us to take to our cabins, and the following three days were anything but pleasant. Finally the sea calmed down, and mother took me up on deck. She pointed to a dark strip on the horizon. It was the Danish coast.

We left the boat at Copenhagen and at once called at the Russian Embassy there, where we were most cordially received. The few hours of our stay in Denmark sufficed to make me love this country, and all my life I have regretted not revisiting it. We returned to the steamer, and played among the rows of oyster baskets for which the St. Petersburg restaurants were anxiously waiting.

Throughout the journey, the Countess Apponyi devoted almost all her time to us children. She was a sweet, beautiful and intelligent woman. The slight cast in her eyes gave her looks a certain indefinite something which increased the charm of her expression. She was the daughter of Count Benckendorff and had married a Hungarian magnate, who was later to play an important part as Austrian Ambassador in London. Many years later, I met her daughter, Countess Borghese.

One day, pressed by our little circle, she sang a Russian romance, "The Nightingale," then a very popular song and one which was often heard in the repertoire of Patti. The countess at the piano made a beautiful picture. Her slender fingers, adorned with rings, fluttered over the keys; her face, framed by her blond hair, glowed with radiance, and her lovely voice touched every heart.

My love for music, to which I gave many hours of my life, dates from that day.

Gradually, the end of our trip approached. In a day we were to land in Kronstadt. But when I arose the next morning, I noticed that the ship was not moving, and soon I was told that we were prevented from docking by a dangerous ice-bar. After a few futile efforts to find a channel, the Captain had to turn around and make a landing in Reval.

There the Countess Apponyi parted from us and continued her journey by carriage to her father's castle. In the meantime, we took a stroll through the streets of the town and along its outskirts. Toward evening, we returned to the boat, and as the ice had floated asunder in the interim, we landed safely in Kronstadt.

My mother's three brothers were at the pier to receive us; they had been very anxious about our delayed landing. With them, we boarded a small steamer and sailed up the Neva toward the Capital. Standing on deck, I saw the gilded domes, the churches and palaces of St. Petersburg approaching nearer and nearer, and I was thrilled at the prospect of finally seeing with my own eyes that city of which I had heard so much.

As soon as we landed, we were surrounded by a crowd of relatives and friends, who embraced and kissed us and, admiring our Paris accents, made us sing little French songs for them. I was greatly awed by Madame Tatyana Potyemkin, my grandmother's sister. She had been a great friend of the Emperor Alexander I, and the Emperor Nicholas I, and made use of these friendships for the purpose of repairing existing wrongs and bad conditions. Among other complaints, she had spoken in behalf of a group of peasants who had lived on her land and who, on account of a revolt, had been banished to Siberia. The ardor of her plea made such a deep impression on the Tsar that he consented to pardon the peasants. As soon as they arrived from Siberia they wanted to thank their patroness, before they reached their home district. In their small sledges, they drew up before my great-aunt's house. Just then, it so happened that the Emperor stepped out of the Winter Palace and the number of miserable vehicles gathered about attracted his attention. When he was informed of the whole business, he immediately called on Madame Potyemkin, whom he found weeping with happiness in the midst of the kneeling peasants. Deeply touched by this scene, the Tsar said: "In the future, I shall pay attention to every plea you make."

My great-aunt was also President of the Committee for Prison Care, which had been founded by Alexander I. She filled this post for thirty years, until her impaired health made it necessary for her to resign. Thus, I seemed to be following a family tradition, when in 1869 I took the same office in obedience to a request of Tsar Alexander III.

Elizabeth Narishkin-Kurakin

The Study of Tsar Nicolai I.

While in St. Petersburg, we lived in the house of my grandmother Galitzine, who was the daughter of the Marshal, Prince Pokrovski, and the widow of Prince Galizin, a grandson of the famous Prince Potyemkin. She was a great lady, distinguished and independent in her views, famous for her lively mind, which was keenly receptive to every stimulus.

After my father had joined us, we started preparations for the big trip across Russia, which was to terminate at my grandfather's domain. What efforts, what patience, and how much time and money were required to make that journey in those days! Today it can be done in thirty-six hours.

We were accommodated in two carriages. The first one was for my parents, while the second carried the children, our Russian nurse and my mother's maid. On specially constructed seats outside of the wagons sat our men-servants. Small wonder that it took ten horses to pull us.

In the broiling heat, we traversed endless roads toward Moscow. Our horses were changed at every station, and we stayed overnight in the cities. We were a thoroughly exhausted party when our carriages finally stopped in front of the house of the Kurakins in Moscow.

This house had originally been a home for disabled soldiers and had been founded at the time by Boris Kurakin in grateful memory of the day that his life was saved at the Battle of Poltava, and here, the respective heads of the family made their domicile. From Moscow, we drove over crude roads again, uphill and downhill, over primitive bridges and out into the plains, and again it seemed an eternity before we reached our destination.

At last we arrived safely at Castle Kurakino and were immediately received by an army of servants. They conducted us through a long suite of rooms into the salon of my grandfather, who at the sight of us, knelt down, and with tears in his eyes said a prayer of thanks for our safe arrival.

My grandfather's life had been a failure. As the only scion of an illustrious name, and heir to a colossal fortune, gifted with spirit and culture, he could have achieved the utmost, had not his egotism and ambition interfered with his success. While still a very young man, he had gone to Paris with his father, who was sent there on a special mission on the occasion of Napoleon's marriage to Marie Louise. At the age of 23 he had married the charming Princess Elizabeth Galizin, a great-granddaughter of the last independent king of Georgia. But he soon began to deceive his young wife and to make her thoroughly unhappy. In her state of mind, and under the influence of a Jesuit priest, she gradually inclined more and more toward the Catholic religion in which she hoped to find solace for her sorrow. But her overwrought nerves were unable to bear the new crisis, and she became a religious maniac at the age of 26. This tragedy darkened the Prince's years forever, as he was well aware of his guilt in the unhappy ending of his wife's life!

Thus my grandfather had gradually developed into an eccentric—a condition manifested by the customs at Castle Kurakino. We did not, for instance, occupy apartments in the castle itself, but in a special house near by, and at a few paces' distance stood a second house, which was occupied by my uncle, Prince Alexander Kurakin, and his young wife. It was entirely because of our visit that my grandfather consented to receive my uncle, for the first time in eight years. Ordinarily, no one was allowed to visit in the castle.

The strange etiquette of this place demanded that we send a messenger to the castle every morning to inquire about the Prince's health. No one was allowed to leave the house until the messenger returned, as this haste might have been interpreted as lack of interest in the well-being of the old gentleman.

During our visit in Kurakino, dinner was served in the castle proper; my father would wear his black clothes, my uncle his uniform, and my mother her most elegant robes.

Although only about a hundred paces separated us from the castle, two four-in-hand carriages were always in attendance to convey us to my grandfather's castle. A cannon was fired off a half-hour before dinner; a second one notified the populace of the fact that dinner was served, and that if they wished to do so, they could say: "Le roi boit."

After dinner, we usually took extensive drives through the beautiful forests and parks of Kurakino. There was a large pond, on which floated boats decorated with banners, and Venetian gondolas, for the manipulation of which there was a corps of oarsmen, dressed in marine uniforms, in readiness. In the middle of the park rose a strangely shaped "Temple of Philosophy," which, for some obscure reason, was surrounded by twelve cannon. It was from these cannon that the signal for dinner was given. At the same time, salutes in honor of the various birthdays in the family were fired from them: twelve salutes for the birthdays of the youngest generation; twenty-four for the parents, and thirty-six for the Prince himself.

My grandfather was a splendid musician. He had his own orchestra which was considered very good. His household consisted mostly of the stewards, secretaries, men and women who read aloud to him, and also of one temporary favorite. These people formed a kind of court state, in which the chief occupation was gossip, intrigue and quarrels. Almost all of them were of low origin and little education, and while they pretended great devotion to and respect for the Prince, gossiped behind his back, and abused his confidence in every way.

Besides the musicians, painters and actors also lived on the estate, for Kurakino Castle had its own theatre where regular performances were staged. They were all serfs, kept to cater to the Prince's whims. In all, they numbered about eight hundred people.

In his declining years, my grandfather often journeyed to Piatigorsk in the Caucasus, to take the baths there. On such occasions, he resembled an Oriental potentate travelling with a whole caravan. His own kitchen, equipped with cooks, scullions and provisions, formed the vanguard; the second vehicle carried toilet articles, vessels, linen and his camp-bed from which my grandfather would never part—it had been given to his uncle by Napoleon. And the august traveler himself was accompanied by a small army of servants, whose number filled several carriages.

CHAPTER II

Back in Paris—On the Eve of the Revolution—Hurrah! Tomorrow We'll Have a Revolution—Stormy Days—The Archbishop of Paris Wounded—The Traces of the Revolution as Seen in the Streets—Russia's Intervention in Hungary—My Father's Acquaintance With Alexandre Dumas—Seances of the Occult Group in the House of the Princess Trubetzkoi—Another Trip to Russia—Anxiety in View of the Imminent Coup D'État in France—Louis Napoleon I or Napoleon III? —The Attitude of Nicholas I—Removal to St. Petersburg.

OUR RETURN to Paris took us over St. Petersburg, Kronstadt, Lübeck, Hamburg, Amsterdam and Antwerp, in those days considered the quickest and most comfortable route. Today I marvel at my mother's courage in undertaking such a trip with four little children. My father, whose leave of absence had expired earlier, had returned to Paris some time before.

We had with us a young tutor who was to teach us Russian. So far we had spoken only French. He was delighted at the opportunity to go to Paris in this capacity; for the Tsar had forbidden Russian students to visit the liberal-minded capital of France. The Emperor Nicholas carried his aversion to the policy of the Citizen-King, Louis Philippe, to such an extent, that he did not even want his country to be represented in Paris. Therefore the Russian diplomatic representation there was headed only by a Chargé d'Affaires, Count von Kisselev. Neither Kisselev nor the other gentlemen of the Legation were married, so that my mother, just as previously, in Vienna, occupied a much more important position within the diplomatic corps than was ordinarily due her.

Besides, family connections facilitated my parents' introduction into French society. One of my mother's cousins had married the Count of Choiseuil, and this connection brought about our subsequent intimate associations with the Duchesses Marnier and FitzJames; we also were in close social contact with the Saint-Priest family. Furthermore, my mother was the only lady of the Russian Colony whom Queen Marie Annette, wife of Louis Philippe, favored with her personal friendship, and as the King was particularly anxious to secure pleasant relations with Russia, my mother became the object of a thousand kind attentions.

We children, too, had a gay, sunny life. Our young Russian tutor gave us our daily lessons in his mother tongue, while the Field-Chaplain, Father Vassileyev, introduced us to the rudiments of the Orthodox faith. We also had an English governess, and took the regular excellent courses of Madame Colart.

It was 1848. Politics were the universal topic of conversation, and while we children were too young to understand what it was all about, still we felt that some important event was in the air. On the eve of the first outbreak, all Paris knew that the next day would bring serious clashes. We were, therefore, forbidden to meet our friends at the Champs Elysées that day, and we, far from being disappointed, shouted jubilantly: "Hurray, tomorrow we'll have a Revolution!" We loved to pronounce this word with its imposing sound, although we had no idea what it meant.

Returning from our walk that day, we stopped in a shop where they sold excellent hot waffles, and our governess said to the shopkeeper: "Of course you'll keep your shop closed, tomorrow."—"No, Madame, on the contrary, we expect a big crowd tomorrow; we are preparing a specially large quantity of batter."

But on the next day, there was no thought of waffles

or of our course at Madame Colart's. The first barricades were being put up, and the crowd was shouting: "Down with Guizot," while here and there the first shots were heard. That evening a concert was to have been given at our house, but of course, neither musicians nor guests arrived. In the meantime, a rumor had it that the rebels had entered some homes, in search of weapons. My father at once decided to bury his small collection of Caucasian swords and hunting-guns in the garden, and we children helped to stamp down the earth diligently, fully convinced that we had been of incalculable aid.

On March 2, 1917, I told Tsar Nicholas II all these details in order to show him from what insignificant beginnings revolutions of historical magnitude can develop. The Tsar, who had just arrived at Tsarskoye Selo, after his abdication, listened to me attentively, and then dropped into deep thought.

My father, who supposed that in those stormy days of 1848, the Russian Embassy would be recalled to St. Petersburg, made preparations for our removal. Instead, however, word came from Russia to remain and await the course of events. Our daily life, in the meantime, had returned to its normal jog, except that our menservants occasionally would appear in the uniform of the National Guard, and that poplars, the trees of liberty, were being planted and dedicated everywhere. Great demonstration parades marched to the City Hall, where their demands, delivered by their speakers, soon melted like snow in the sunshine under the oratorical bombast of Lamartine. By virtue of his oratorical talent, Lamartine was the only man who was able to preserve any sort of order. If he had had the misfortune to become hoarse just once, a new overthrow might have followed, for the power of the Provisional Government was nil.

During our walks we often encountered wagons on which white-robed women enacted living pictures, trying to represent one or another of the civic virtues. Child that I was, it seemed to me that nothing could possibly be so wonderful as to be one of those ladies, shivering with cold in her tarlatan dress.

Months of comparative quiet were followed by new clashes which, this time, were more violent and bloody. The entire male population of Paris fought at the Barricades, for one side or another, the air was vibrant with gunfire, all shops were closed, and in front of the houses women were shredding lint for bandages. Several Russian families fled to our Embassy and were sheltered there as well as it was possible.

Suddenly the rumor spread that the Archbishop of Paris, Monseigneur Affre, had been wounded at the Barricades. It was true that the venerable Prince of the Church had appeared, with the cross raised in his hand, at the arena of the most violent fighting and had, despite the danger, tried to stop the combatants from committing murder. A stray bullet had wounded him, and his fall made such a deep impression on both camps, that hostilities were stopped.

After the rebellion had completely broken down, my mother took us with her to see what damage had been done in the streets, particularly in the Faubourg St. Antoine; here ambulances were stationed at every street corner, and crowds of wounded men surrounded them.

A few weeks later, we left for Dieppe, where a numerous contingent of Paris society had gathered to recuperate from the excitement of the days of horror. Naturally, everybody talked politics, and not only those of local interest, for all of Europe was in rebellion. Among the many friends of my parents was also the Princess Mombard, mother of King Karl Albert, who was just then fighting Austria in order to liberate Piedmont from the Hapsburg rule. The princess looked like a trooper. She was tall and stout, and boasted a prominent, graying moustache. I believe that she was a very clever conversationalist, to judge from the demand there was for her society.

The approaching elections held everyone's attention. Each of the candidates outdid the other in hymning his own party's praise and caricaturing that of the other. I can still remember a lampoon which caused some amusement in those days: it represented Prince Louis Napoleon battling with an eagle which was trying to snatch his hat away.

The Russian Empire was the only European country of any consequence that had not been shaken by the Revolution, and when in the following year, the Hungarian Rebellion threatened Austria's existence, Tsar Nicholas I made the great mistake of sending his army to aid the House of Hapsburg. He thus antagonized Hungary and at the same time supported the same Austrian party which was later to place obstacles before all Russian politics regarding the Eastern question. Little did we then know what damaging consequences this intervention would have; at the time we were proud to see Russia take a decisive action in a West European situation.

We spent the summer of 1849 on the charming estate of Villeneuve l'Étang, at Marne. Never have I seen more beautiful trees nor a more luxuriant vegetation than in the park of that Castle; marvelous tulips grew there and magnolias, and wonderful old nut-trees. A rock in the middle of the pond was covered with red-flowering plants and bushes and all around the lake circled a path hemmed in by colorful flowers; strawberries and mushrooms grew in profusion everywhere.

Our greatest pleasure that summer consisted in going to all the festivals in the vicinity of Paris, of which the jolliest was held at Saint Cloud. There was a whole row of booths in which one could buy toys, barley-sugar candy and other sweets. Cooks in white aprons and caps prepared appetizing dishes in the open air and tried to attract the public's attention by cries and ringing of bells.

These amusements were more to my taste in those days than the interesting literary associations which my father had in the meantime made. He had paid a visit to the famous Alexandre Dumas in his Castle Monte Cristo near Saint Cloud and had met Monsieur and Madame Lamartine. Father had also begun to show a great interest in Occult Science, which was then the fashionable fad, and so I often heard them talk of somnambulists like Alexis Didier. My mother, however, did not like this subject and always tried to keep it from the ears of us children.

Very often, father attended seances in the house of the Princess Trubetzkoi. This invalid lady, who left her chaise longue very rarely, saw in these experiments a welcome diversion and was happy to have found such a fascinating entertainment for her evenings.

In the following year, we took another trip to Russia, but this time, a sad event was the immediate cause of our going. My uncle, Prince Sergei Galitzine, had been fatally wounded at a shooting party and my grandmother's sorrow was very great. My mother felt that her place was with her now, and that her presence might help to console her, and so my father let us all go. This time we traveled by way of Dunkirk and our trip was undisturbed and uneventful.

We spent the summer with my grandmother in Pavlovsk, where several other relatives were in attendance on her. The arrival of my aunt, Maria Kurakin, and her three children, who were welcome playmates, made our visit perfect. We enjoyed trips to the islands near St. Petersburg, where the Kurakins lived in a beautiful house with a big garden.

Once we called on my Aunt Potyemkin in Gastilitsa. Hers was a splendid estate, on which my uncle had built a luxurious castle equipped with every modern comfort of that era. They repeatedly entertained the Emperor and the Empress there, and played the host to many foreign princes. As my grandfather had gone to the Caucasus for his usual season, we did not stop at Castle Kurakino. The old Prince died en route, while we were already halfway to Paris. He left a colossal fortune, but his affairs were so complicated that it took years before all questions of inheritance were settled.

The following summer saw us again at Villeneuve l'Étang, where this time we received many guests. The Princess Kutusov and the Countess Branier de St. Simon, cousins of my mother, came often, and we played a good deal of music. Sometimes the Princess Dondukov, whose husband later became Russian Minister of the Exterior, entered our circle. I once played for her, and she was greatly surprised at my command of expression, considering my youth.

One of my greatest delights in those days was to go horseback riding with my brothers. During the following summer, which we spent in St. Germain, we often rode as far as Chillon du Val, to call on the Princess de Pair, or we galloped to Poiny, where we usually attended to some errands. In between, we played at amateur theatricals, which entertained us hugely.

It had gradually become very evident that Prince Louis Napoleon, the President of the Republic, desired the title of Emperor, a situation which gave rise to much anxiety regarding French foreign politics. My parents were often the guests of Louis Napoleon, and it was there that they met the Countess Montijo and her daughter, the future Empress Eugenie.

The Russian Chargé d'Affaires, Count Kisselev, had been called to Russia to report to Secretary of State Nesselrode. In his absence, my father managed the affairs of the Embassy, and tried everything in his power to please President Napoleon. The diplomatic circles of the time discussed with much gusto whether the new ruler would call himself Louis Napoleon I or, as successor to the Corsican and the Duke of Reichstadt, Napoleon III. The Austrian Ambassador, Baron Hübner, declared at the time that his Government would never acknowledge a Napoleon III, although subsequent events proved that Austrian politics could always adapt themselves to new conditions, and that their leaders were always ready to sacrifice their principles to a temporary advantage.

Entirely different was Russia's reaction. Tsar Nicholas regarded himself as the embodiment of the absolutistic principle. He had just saved Austria from collapse, and now believed that, as monarch by Divine Right, he could impress his will on all of Europe, and that he need not consider any opposition. Diplomacy seemed to him—the simple honest soldier—unnecessary; it only served to artificially obscure perfectly clear situations. In my opinion, it was this viewpoint of the Tsar that brought about all the serious mistakes which terminated in the fatal Crimean war. Count Nesselrode tried in vain to evade all complications, and to preserve the status quo. The Emperor declared flatly that he regarded himself the protector of all Christians . . . a remark which led to a conflict, not only with the Holy See, but with Austria and Turkey as well.

After the successful coup d'etat of December 2nd,

and the restoration of the French Empire, the question arose as to what degree the European powers would consider the new ruler their equal. The Emperor of Austria was the first to address Napoleon as "Brother," but Tsar Nicholas refused to do this and persisted to regard him only as "Friend." This circumstance was, in the end, responsible for the misfortune that, on the eve of a great war, Russia lost France as an ally.

A great change began to take place in our private life, as my father had been offered the post of Ambassador to Lisbon. At the same time, my mother, to her profound astonishment, received a proposal to become court lady to the Grand Duchess Helen and her daughter Katharina, wife of the Duke of Mecklenburg, in St. Petersburg, . . . an offer which surprised my mother the more as, while in Paris, we had had no relations with the St. Petersburg Court.

The complicated testamentary arrangements of my grandfather made the presence of my parents in Russia necessary on that account alone, and so it was decided to break up our Paris domicile and move to St. Petersburg. The thought of leaving Paris, where I had spent all my childhood, and to which I was attached by a thousand lovely memories, made me sad; at the same time, the prospect of living in my own country which, discounting my two visits, I did not know at all, transported me into something of patriotic enthusiasm.

We left on June 23, 1853. I remember the day well, and I see our dear house distinctly before me, as we left it; I knew that I should never see it again.

CHAPTER III

We Settle in Russia—The Life of the Grand-Duchess Helen—My First Visit to Our Country Estate—The Crimean War—Death of Emperor Nicholas I—The Liberation of the Peasants—Cruel Effects of Serfdom—I am Presented to the Empress—Trip to Nice and Rome—An Official Visit in Paris—Reception by Empress Eugenie—The Tsar at the Costume Ball—The Salon of the Grand-Duchess Helen—What is a Nihilist?—

MY PARENTS had decided to settle in Russia permanently. We took a large apartment at the Mars Field which was splendid enough, but very uncomfortable as to the arrangement of rooms as well as to their temperature, which was almost always zero. My father had been guided in the choice of the apartment by the adaptability of its wall space to his paintings and other objects of art which he had brought from Paris; the thought of comfort for daily life was negligible to him.

It was no small task for my mother to rearrange our life and to revive friendly and family connections interrupted for fourteen years. The Palais Michael became the center of her social activities. It was there that the Grand Duchess Helen had opened her beautiful home of which she was herself the brightest star. She promptly recognized and appreciated the new mental stimulus which my mother brought to her salon. The latter had spent her entire youth in diplomatic circles, in the focus of ideas which radiated beyond the usual horizon. What wonder she shone brilliantly, and easily adapted herself to a new circle which was the only one among the aristocracy in St. Petersburg, worthy of the name salon . . . as salons used to be in the old days in Paris.

The Grand Duchess Helen was also actively interested in our education, and particularly in the courses we had taken with Colart and his successor Remy. We had to show our lessons and books to her Lady-of-Honor, and undergo a sort of examination. The Grand Duchess had long cherished the dream of improving the education of women in Russia, and had given orders to Mlle. Troubat in Paris, the former governess of her daughter, the Grand Duchess Katharina, to report to St. Petersburg on everything interesting in that respect. Within a short time, the courses of Mlle. Troubat had become fashionable in St. Petersburg, and were frequented by all the young girls of our society, thanks to the support and encouragement of the Grand Duchess. Later, the Empress herself organized Grammar Schools for the masses, for which there was an urgent need.

The Grand Duchess Helen was a remarkable personality, whose biography ought to be written. It would not fail to interest a great many people. She was born as a Princess of Würtemberg and lost her mother early. At the beginning of the Restoration she lived with her father and sister in Paris. Her father, the brilliant Prince Paul, liked Paris, with its intellectual and artistic circles which, compared to his limited little German Court, pleased his fastidious mind infinitely better. When, sometime later, he was requested to return to Stuttgart in order to give his daughters the education due to their position, he refused to go. He claimed not to have the means to bring up his daughters as princesses. On the contrary, he found that he would have to send them to an institution (not the usual thing for Princesses). He actually did. And so the two princesses formed curious associations. They met a Miss Walter at the institute, who was related to the great Cuvier, and at whose house all important intellectuals of those days used to meet. Every Sunday evening, gatherings were held there, which not only the two princesses but their father too would regularly attend. The older of the two girls, the later Grand Duchess Helen, listened eagerly to the fascinating and brilliant conversations there, and thus laid the foundation for her later remarkable development of mind. All this took place in the modest rooms of the Cuvier apartment, situated near the Botanical Garden, and the Princesses sewed with their own hands the little white dresses which they wore on those evenings. Later, these reminiscences sounded strangely from the lips of the wealthy and brilliant Grand Duchess who carried her high rank with such dignity.

At the beginning, her life as Grand Duchess was not easy, although the Emperor and Empress were kindly disposed toward her. She remained childless, and the Empress, sensitive and sympathetic soul that she was, suffered with her under that affliction.

This gentle Empress found herself pushed into the background by the Emperor's mother, who, surrounded by the adulation of her sons, continued to play the most important part with their consent, and showered all her favors on the Grand Duchess Nicholas who was the daughter of Queen Louise of Prussia and who already boasted of an heir.

What the warm-hearted young Grand Duchess Helen needed and what she so sadly missed was the happiness of reciprocal affection; but the Grand Duke Michael, her husband, made no effort to disguise his coldness to her. He was a soldier first and last, and devoted to the army with body and soul. This loneliness of heart, and her fruitless efforts toward a closer union with her husband, made the life of the young matron dreary and sad. Not one of her cherished dreams was to be realized!

Crown Prince Alexander Nicolayevich in the year 1833

Alexânder II as Crown Prince

Grand Duchess Alexandra Alexandrovna

She told us one day, how she was once seated at one of the windows of the Winter Palace, looking out on the turbid, cold waves of the Neva, as they rolled on to the sea. She thought how much her life resembled this grey river, moving along as joylessly . . . and at this moment she wished she could be carried out on those leaden waves and disappear with them into the sea. Just then the Emperor Alexander entered. She tried to avert her tear-stained face, and the Tsar, pretending not to have noticed anything, sat down next to her and told her, with touching delicacy, intimate details of his life, his suffering, his cares and hopes. At the end, he said that the lot of those chosen by God for exalted positions was to sacrifice their personal wishes to their duty.

"We do not belong to ourselves," he concluded. "We are tools in the hands of God, destined to fulfill His will; we are the means He has chosen. Our happiness consists in following His call; only thus can we do good."

The Grand Duchess used to add that she was not sure that she fully understood the meaning of those words then. But she clearly felt that in that moment, her life had been decisively affected. Is it not a beautiful picture to contemplate this man who had tasted all honors, distinctions and also all the troubles of this earth, in conversation with a child at the threshold of life, one might say, teaching her how to continue it with dignity?

The Grand Duchess Helen was very kind to us little girls; she invited us and our mothers to the celebration of Easter eve, one Spring. Since her husband's death she had refrained from celebrating it with the Imperial family in the Winter Palace. On that night, she preferred to stay home with her daughter, the Grand Duchess Katharina. The magnificent character of this reception made a deep impression on me. After the Mass, all the servants of the Palace—their number was legion—and their wives gathered around the tables laden with dishes, to taste food for the first time after a long fast. The priest, followed by the Grand Duchess, walked from table to table sprinkling the food with holy water. Behind him walked the Groom of the Chambers, carrying a large vessel filled with china eggs, which the Grand Duchess distributed as she passed.

In the Spring, the Grand Duchesses left for their summer palace in Kamenoi-Ostrov, while we remained in town a little longer.

In the beginning of July, we, too, went to our country estate where my father and brothers were expecting us. The railway trip there seemed endless to us, and indeed it was very long. But we quickly forgot our discomforts and hardships when our valet announced that Father had come to meet us at the border with our carriages. Soon we were in his arms. My brothers, the steward, and some peasants in red shirts accompanied him. The peasants had brought salt and bread as a symbol of welcome. My mother was placed in father's carriage, Boris jumped into ours, and as we sped along the road, he explained everything and told me that a horse was waiting for me in the stable.

Our tired horses had to exert all their remaining strength to make the short distance to the house at a gallop. We skirted a large pond as big as a lake on which was moored a yacht bearing our coat-of-arms. Driving through the park we passed the orangery, and finally we stood in the court of honor.

A large crowd waited there to welcome us. It was a moment of mutual joy, a flush of popularity which took me by surprise. My mother's wedding had taken place on this estate, and she had visited it once after that. The people had learned to know and love her, and now they were thanking God with fervent voices for having sent her back to them. We children had our share of the prevailing festive spirit and were greatly moved by it.

For the first time in my life I felt the powerful charm of home and country. I had not felt this in St. Petersburg, where everything had seemed beautiful, certainly, but also cold and formal. The impression which our ancestral home made on me has never faded and the word home is always associated in my mind with our estate, Stepanovski. Much of my life's work went toward its improvement. On the other hand, when the Revolution ruined our estate and menaced our lives, I received from the people of Stepanovski many proofs of their undiminished loyalty, and many demonstrations of the strength of those ties which had bound our family to this piece of earth for three hundred years.

Upon that first visit to our estate, Father conducted us through the drawing rooms, the library and the picture gallery, and we followed him in awed wonder. Great crystal bowls filled with luscious fruit stood everywhere, and we were overjoyed when he said: "Eat children, eat; it is all for you."

Upon our return to St. Petersburg, we found everyone depressed and sad. At times, there was even open muttering and grumbling. This was a new phenomenon. So far, the name of Tsar Nicholas had been surrounded by an aura of infallibility; now there was general dissatisfaction, which was increasingly aggravated by political complications with foreign powers.

The Grand Duchess Helen was the only one who did not join in this futile chorus of complaints. She, rather, developed a beneficent practical activity. No sooner had she discovered the sad state of our military hospitals than she thought of the heavy human sacrifice the war would demand. She immediately organized a private aid society for the wounded. It was her boundless influence with the Emperor that made it possible for her to have the first group of Sisters of Charity at her command, despite the objections of the military administration.

The Emperor himself suffered unspeakably from the failure of his political tactics. His life's work seemed to be crumbling before him. Both his pride and his faith as a good Christian had been deeply hurt. His disappointment at the unhappy outcome of the Crimean War was so great that even *his* iron constitution could not bear the moral breakdown which ensued. He died February 18, 1855, leaving to his son, Alexander II, the burden of an unfortunately waged war and a shaken empire.

The siege of Sebastopol with its accompaniment of unspeakable suffering and unparalleled heroism was protracted until April 26th of that year, when the city was finally evacuated. This was followed by the Peace of Paris, and then the coronation of the new ruler began to occupy the popular mind. It was solemnly celebrated exactly one year after the surrender of Sebastopol.

By the end of these festivities, the new Emperor had delivered his celebrated address to the assembled aristocracy, proclaiming his intention of doing away with serfdom, and he called upon them to assist him in this great work.

The Grand Duchess Helen was one of the first to answer the call. She immediately worked out a project for the liberation of her peasants on her estate in Karlovka in the Government of Poltava; but although a few other landowners imitated her, the good work could only be achieved by legislative measures. This finally was accomplished by the famous Act of February 19, 1861.

Young as I was, the thought of a human being as the property of another had always revolted me, and I had always detested the gauging of our landed proprietors' wealth by the number of "souls" they owned. At that time I did not even know to what brutal degree the masters often misused their rights; but even the normal condition of the serfs seemed shameful to me.

My mother, for instance, owned an estate in the Government of Tula with many serfs—industrious people—many of whom had come to St. Petersburg and who by paying a stipulated annual indemnity, were allowed to work at whatever they liked. Among them were some who had grown rich by trade, and had even bought some property. But, according to law, as serfs they could not own real estate, so that all the necessary formalities had to be transacted in my mother's name, who figured in all the documents as the owner of the properties. It is obvious to what abuses such a condition could lead, if, for instance, the master had no intention of being honest, or if he suddenly died, and his heirs took his place. The real owners of the property had no other proof of their ownership than the word of their masters.

The following is a typical case:

An old lady, living in seclusion on her estate, had attached to herself a young girl serf gifted with a remarkable musical talent. She grew very fond of this girl and treated her as her own daughter, even arranging for the girl's tuition in all cultural branches. As she had neither children nor close relatives of her own, she decided to adopt the girl and leave everything to her.

One day, upon returning home from a picnic, the child found her foster mother paralyzed by a stroke. The old lady died without regaining consciousness and without having been able to put her generous intentions into legal form. Thus the hitherto gently bred girl, the foster child of a lady, was left destitute and a serf. The fortune was transferred to a distant relative of the deceased who had never even visited the old lady but had, when necessary, sent his steward. The girl had to return to the village in which she was registered, to resume her dull life in the midst of peasants. One can easily understand what the child suffered.

Fortunately this incident occurred in the year 1860, so that the unhappy girl was soon released from her unpleasant surroundings, the abrogation of serfdom giving her her liberty. With her nephew, who also was musically gifted, she went to Moscow and earned her living by giving music lessons. Later the nephew organized a church choir, which I heard on one occasion at Madame Abaza's. The "Missa Papae Marcelli" of Palestrina as sung by this choir made a deep impression on me. Amid the celebrated guests I noticed in the audience a woman of about forty years, who attracted my attention because of her simple black silk dress. She followed the Latin words of the choir lovingly, forming them in advance with her lips, as if she knew the text by heart. Later, when I inquired about her, I was given her story, which I have just told.

By 1857, I had already begun to be passionately interested in literature. I remember how I devoured Lermontov's "Demon," which was as yet circulating in manuscript only. My plethora of emotion had to find an outlet, which it did by pouring my soul into poetry and a diary. My family gave me little encouragement in this. My mother accused me of indifference to our family life, saying: "You act like a misunderstood genius."

But when, in the autumn of 1858, I was presented to the Empress, she greeted me with the words: "Is it you, my child, who writes such pretty verses?" I became embarrassed and answered in confusion: "They are nothing, Your Majesty."

"Indeed," she replied with a smile, "I have heard them well praised."

My small emotional effusions had actually become well known and sometimes my dancing partners would recite a line or two of them to me. It seems that my father had secretly copied some of my verses and showed them to his friends, whence they had found their way to the Empress.

I spent the following winter in the South, as the Grand Duchess Katharina was ill and had asked me to accompany her as her Lady-in-Waiting. We went to Nice, and I marvelled at the tropical vegetation of that sunny spot which at that time still belonged to Italy.

Among the people we met at Nice, I noticed particularly Prince Volkonski, a pardoned Dekabrist, who was living there with this wife. She was one of those Dekabrist wives who had followed her husband voluntarily into exile, and to my romantic mind she was surrounded by a halo of heroism and martyrdom.

I also made the acquaintance of Vassili Chicherin, the Secretary of the Embassy, who had just become engaged to a Baroness Meyendorff. His son became a follower of the revolutionary movement and is now famous as leader of the foreign political affairs of Soviet Russia.

In the beginning of 1859, we made an unforgettable journey to Rome; from there we sailed to Civitavecchia and thence to Marseilles. In Marseilles, a surprise awaited us. M. Novitzki, the Russian military plenipotentiary in Paris, met us with a long telegram from the Grand Duchess Helen to her daughter, urgently requesting her to stop at Paris and pay an official visit to the Tuileries. For the Emperor Napoleon was said to have remarked to the Ambassador, Count Kisselev, that among the many Russian Princesses passing through Paris on their way to the Riviera, not one had thought it worth her while to stop and pay her respects to the Empress Eugenie. Napoleon, the telegram continued, had let it be understood that he considered this a breach of etiquette.

It was on the eve of the war with Austria, and while our Emperor had no intention of interfering, still he wished to maintain friendly relations with France and to keep Napoleon's temper unruffled. He had therefore expressed the wish that the Grand Duchess Katharina pay a formal visit to the Empress Eugenie.

The telegram fell upon the Grand Duchess Katharina like a thunderbolt. She was in the eighth month of her pregnancy, and felt herself incapable of undergoing the hardships of such a visit in her condition. Besides, her husband, the Duke of Mecklenburg, doubted the wisdom of his appearance in Paris at this time, considering his German nationality and his alliance with Austria. The not unimportant question of dress, too, loomed up as a difficulty in the present situation, and finally there was the possibility of Napoleon's being too busy with preparations for war to receive us. We then decided to let my mother and Prince Meshcherski travel on ahead, to discuss the details of this visit with Count Kisselev in Paris. In the meantime, the Grand Duchess, pending directions, was to travel leisurely through the South of France. It was in Lyons that my mother's telegram reached us, indicating that the presence of the Grand Duchess was desired.

In Paris we were received by the members of the Russian Colony, and introduced to the party whom the French Court had assigned to attend the Grand Duchess. State carriages awaited us and took us to the Tuileries, where we were received by the Empress and the Princesses Clothilde and Mathilde and King Jerome, the brother of Napoleon. After the usual presentations, I was taken to the apartment reserved for me—a beautiful big bedroom with a connecting drawing room whose windows and balcony overlooked the Garden of the Tuileries.

The following three days were a succession of visits and drives to the Louvre and the Bois de Boulogne. Of the three state dinners, two were given by the Empress and one by Count Kisselev. The Empress was charming. She evidently had slipped easily and with dignity into her new position as Empress. She had a lovely figure and shoulders, and knew how to conduct a conversation with ease and grace.

We saw some of our old friends and acquaintances again; then we left Paris early in the morning. In Verviers, at the border, we separated. The Grand Duchess Katharina went to Mecklenburg while we went to Spa, where I intended to take the waters, and where we met the Grand Duchess Maria, and her charming daughters. Together we traveled to Remplin in Mecklenburg, a beautiful estate, to see the Grand Duchess Katharina. Soon we were joined by the Grand Duchess Helen and her entire court. After a short stay in Bad Doberan, we finally went to Wismar, where we boarded a battleship which had been placed at the disposal of the Grand Duchess for her return trip to Russia.

Toward the end of August, we were back at Oranienbaum and had resumed our usual social life. Drives alternated with concerts, theatrical performances, charades and balls in the Palace of the Grand Duchess. Late in the fall, we visited Gachina for two weeks, where all sorts of diversions were arranged for us with truly royal luxury and the highest artistic refinement. Those were the days when the magnificence of the Russian Court was unequalled.

At the beginning of the winter the Grand Duchess

Helen gave her gala masked ball, which the Tsar attended, dressed in a domino. In order not to be recognized, he asked a number of gentlemen who resembled him in stature, to wear dominoes also and to imitate his manner as closely as possible. The loosening of social barriers, due to the carnival spirit, brought about many a discussion of political questions that night, which the Tsar, who joined them incognito, hugely enjoyed.

In those days the salon of the Grand Duchess Helen was the center of all intellectual life. It was an era rich in eminent men, and all the outstanding minds found in the Grand Duchess an encouraging and stimulating patroness. At her Thursday evenings she received all the shining lights of arts and science. Even the Emperor liked to be present. One continued chatting in his presence, or one listened to some excellently rendered music, while the young people were gay with all sorts of games.

St. Petersburg society, however, was far from unanimously approving of the Grand Duchess Helen. There was one party which was quite inimical to her and the Grand Duke Konstantin, and she was openly accused of undermining the foundations of the Empire and the property rights of the aristocracy. It was true that the Grand Duke was often abrupt and unpleasant, and that he made no secret of his contempt for the high aristocracy. Nor did he hesitate to show his sympathy with democratic ideas.

The Grand Duchess Katharina and I read a good deal together, at that time. I remember reading Turgenyev's "Fathers and Sons" to her, and we came across the word "nihilist." She asked me what it meant, but I was unable to explain. That word, invented by Turgenyev, which later became so well known, was then just as unknown as the doctrine for which it was to stand.

My father had just passed through a great sorrow,

which came to him through the death of my brother Boris. He had been his pride and joy. After weeks of despondency, I was happy to see that my father was trying to find consolation in religion, and I translated a number of beautiful old Slavic prayers which, though he did not understand them, he loved. When the liberation of the serfs was proclaimed, he drove to his estate in person to read the manifesto to his peasants. Later, at the time of the division of the land, he proved very generous to them and considered their advantage only. This kindness laid the foundation for the loyal relationship which existed between us and our peasants, and which lasted even through the great Revolution.

During our mourning, the Grand Duchess Helen was so kind to me, that I wondered how she could devote so much time and thought to a young girl. She soon noticed that I was in no mood to seek society, and so she suggested that I take up some serious work. She had founded a home for aged women, which for some reason was, at that moment, without management, and he asked me to accept its directorship.

My family had always laughed at my lack of practical sense, and so my first reaction to the proposal was a feeling of inadequacy for the post. Nevertheless, after some hesitation, I took up the direction of the home and, to my surprise, found myself getting along famously. Whenever I encountered difficulties, I consulted Madame Von Rahden at first, but soon the Grand Duchess asked me to come to her directly, and talk over my difficulties with her. She always received me alone, and after solving my problems with a few words, would ask many questions concerning my private life. I could not but answer frankly; and she told me about herself, and said words to me which I have never forgotten.

CHAPTER IV

The Literary Salon of the Countess Tolstoy—My Acquaintanceship with Dostoyevski—Dostoyevski's Reading at My House — Dostoyevski as Actor — The Poet-Philosopher —Solovyev—His First Lecture at the University—Solovyev on Schopenhauer—Acquaintanceship with Anatole Fyodorovich Koni—The Literary Salon of the Grand Duchess of Leuchtenberg—The Minister of Finance as Novelist—Goncharov's Critical Remark.

IN 1875 a new element came into my life through my acquaintanceship with the members of the literary circle which collected around the Countess Sophia Andreyevna Tolstoy, the widow of the poet, Alexei Tolstoy. The Countess had come to St. Petersburg after her husband's death, about a year before, and I had met her casually. She now began to receive regularly on Mondays, and I, with my friends, the Countesses Baryatinski and Volkonski, accepted her invitation for these evenings with great pleasure. Within a short time I was completely captivated by the charm of her intelligence, her culture, and the fine critical talent which she displayed in her conversations about literature and music.

There was only one feature of her character which displeased me. This was her eclectic philosophy, which made it impossible to recognize to what religion or to what philosophical system she belonged. She always agreed with everyone and had a clever way of picking out of other people's ideas, certain corresponding viewpoints which she then deftly combined into an opinion. In her salon, dimly lighted by shaded lamps and scented with a strong odor of hyacinths, with Hindu idols gleam-

*The Poet-Philospher Solovyev.

ing from dark recesses, the Countess talked with equally dispassionate objectiveness about all creeds.

Once, when the Countess Volkonski and I were waiting for our carriages after we had left the Countess Tolstoy's home, we looked at each other silently.

"What do you think?" I finally asked.

Whereupon the Countess Volkonski answered pensively:

"There is an intoxicating, poisonous atmosphere up there! One not firm in his faith may well beware!"

These words of Elizaveta Georgyevna expressed my feelings exactly.

I was not sure enough of myself to engage in an open discussion with the Countess, yet I did not want to create the impression that I fully agreed with her. Therefore I was very glad to find her alone one day. With great warmth and conviction, I unfolded my confession of faith to her. She listened calmly, and then simply said:

"How strongly developed your bump of reverence is!"

Much as I was piqued by her derisive remark, I was satisfied to have declared my opinion about these questions once and for all.

One fact, however, must be admitted: as soon as one had crossed the threshold of the Salon Tolstoy, one shed all gossip and small talk. The friends of her deceased husband, who continued their friendly relations with the widow, formed the main circle of these meetings. And so here I regularly met Goncharov, Polonski, Maikov, Markevitch, Dostoyevski and sometimes Turgenyev, when he happened to be in St. Petersburg.

Needless to say, this literary circle was a great attraction to me. To be able to associate with authors whose spirit I already knew through their works, and who had become dear to me, exercised a particular charm over me. I was interested in Dostoyevski more than in any other.

It seemed to me that he always wore a thorny crown of sorrows, those sorrows which lifted his soul beyond terrestrial life and gave him that clairvoyance and merciful understanding for other people's troubles.

Dostoyevski preferred to address himself to one single person, and even when he participated in the conversation of a whole group, he gradually turned to one individual and continued the conversation with him alone. As his soft voice would grow still lower and the eyes in his lean, pale face glowed still deeper, his conversation, too, became more intense and significant. It was at that time that he was working on his "Brothers Karamazov." One day he told me that he was filled with horror at what he was yet to write, for he lived through all the woe and sorrow of his characters, not as if in imagination, but with the acuteness of reality. He told me too—and with deep earnestness—about his being condemned to death, and about the unexpected pardon which was announced to him as he mounted the steps to the gallows. He told it so graphically, that the cold shivers ran down my spine.

Although he rather fled from than sought people, he was so kind as to participate in a musical and literary soirée which I had arranged for a charitable purpose. With compelling artistry he read his charming novel, "The Boy's Christmas Eve With Christ," and the audience stormed with enthusiasm when he recited Pushkin's "Prophet," an unusual demonstration from this mundane, elegant group which had gathered at my house that night. Dostoyevski's usually bent figure, seemed suddenly to grow with the force of the rhythm. He stood erect: his eyes flashed. His ordinarily timid voice became strong and rang out powerfully. It was evident that he had undergone a complete change.

Shortly before his death, he expected to face the public once more at my house. We had intended to perform a few scenes from Alexei Tolstoy's "Ivan the Terrible." Prince Ivan Michailovitch Galitzine was to play the part of the Emperor, while Dostoyevski was to play the Eremite.

Unfortunately, we were not to enjoy this performance. Dostoyevski became ill of a fatal malady which ended a life fraught with storms and sorrow. His funeral was a truly great event. All of St. Petersburg, including every class of people, took part in it.

At one of the Countess Tolstoy's evenings, I also met the poet-philosopher, Vladimir Sergeyevich Solovyev, and his friend, Prince Dimitri Zeretelli. They had only recently appeared in society. Both were interested in philosophy and poetry, although Solovyev surpassed the Prince in education and intelligence. Soon these inseparable friends became steady callers at my house as well as those of the Countess Baryatinski and the Countess Volkonski—the Triumvirate, as we three friends were called.

Solovyev was a man of remarkable appearance. His pale, regular features were framed by thick, black wavy hair. His forehead was lofty, like that of a thinker, his eyes were blue, and an almost horizontal line of eyebrows cut straight across the upper part of his face. This upper part was so perfect and so pure, that it made one think, involuntarily, of the Saviour, for a picture of Whom he would have made a splendid model. But the lower part of his face expressed an unpleasant sensuality, which even his flowing beard could not entirely obscure. This beard had a queer way of jutting out whenever Solovyov laughed. Many found this laughter charming and naive, but I thought it a little repellent and rude. This face corresponded exactly to its owner's character, for Solovyov was as much a man of mystic idealism as one of lusty materialism. It is true that his idealism usually predominated, but not without many a hard battle.

His voice was wonderfully harmonious and his speech, which he often embellished with verses, flattered the emotions and the imagination. He had just been made Professor of Theology and Philosophy and his brilliant lectures attracted masses of young students of all subjects; they created almost a revolution, and a general interest in intellectual work. We were present at his introductory lecture at the University and religiously attended the courses which he gave later in the "Salyanoi Gorodok," the Latin Quarter of St. Petersburg.

He used to speak there on philosophic and theological subjects, and concluded them with his definition of the "God-Man." His words impressed his audience enormously and people flocked to his lectures. Very interesting was his analysis of Schopenhauer's Pessimism, to which he added the remark that this doctrine had developed in Europe during the time of the greatest prosperity. This, he said, proved the eternal incapability of the human soul for finding complete satisfaction in earthly possessions. When he spoke on philosophical ideas, the beauty and lucidity of his exposition was entrancing and incomparable.

He did not impress me thus when he talked of theological matters. There the strong influence of the Alexandrian School made itself noticeable and, according to my impressions, he drifted too often into a vague Neo-Platonism and Pantheism.

It was really a strange sight to see our sober St. Petersburg public listening to discussions on such remote subjects. I believe that much of what Solovyev said was beyond the understanding of many. But he lifted one into unknown spiritual heights and impressed one much

Tsarina Maria Alexandrovna, Wife of Alexander II

Tsar Alexander II

in the same manner as Wagner's music did at that same time.

It was in the salon of the Grand Duchess Eugenia Maximilianovna that I made another interesting acquaintance about that time—the eminent jurist, Anatole Fyodorovich Koni. He was then still highly esteemed and the Countess Pahlen, especially, received him most cordially in her home. The Count, too, thought very well of him, and the Countess even asked him to lecture to her daughters and their circle of friends on the elements of law. Koni was delighted with this proposal. Unfortunately, however, he did not lecture with much enthusiasm. Neither the atmosphere nor the preparatory training and attention of the young students were of a nature to inspire the lecturer to a serious treatment of his subject.

The Grand Duchess Leuchtenberg used to receive the most eminent personages on regular evenings. These soirées were very pleasant. Stasilyevitch used to come very often with his first literary efforts which he allowed us to enjoy from the manuscript before they were published. Koni, too, read beautifully. Afterwards at the supper table lively discussions and interesting talks about the absorbing events of the day would ensue. The critical opinions I used to hear there were so brilliant in form and content that I was enchanted and felt myself transplanted into new spiritual worlds.

During the season the Grand Duchess, who was in mourning, and so did not attend parties, left for Peterhof. She invited us to join her there for a visit and the little excursion proved to be a most delightful experience. The evening before, we had attended a ball in the Palace of the Grand Duke Vladimir Alexandrovich. After the artificial atmosphere of this Court function, conducted in the most luxurious style, we were transported with delight to find ourselves suddenly on a crisp winter morning driving through snowfields and trees glistening with hoarfrost, to the quiet estate where the Grand Duchess had—like Marie-Antoinette at the Trianon—surrounded herself with an elegant, tasteful, but costly simplicity.

At the above-mentioned ball of the Grand Duke Vladimir Alexandrovich, the Minister of the Imperial Treasury, Peter Alexandrovich Valuyev, asked me what had become of the novel I had written. Not in the least abashed, I inquired about his novel, which, I knew, he had read to the Princess Paskevich. After our little chat, the Minister of the Imperial Treasury consented to read his work to me and also to the Countess Baryatinski. From that time on, we took turns in meeting alternately at the house of the Princess and at my own.

Valuyev's novel was excellently written, but the stilted dialogue of his dramatis personae was a bit dull. Goncharov, whose opinion Valuyev sought, expressed himself adversely regarding the artificial aristocracy of the subject, and the author's complete indifference to the lower classes. This indifference, said Goncharov, went so far, that only the aristocracy existed for Valuyev; for he never mentioned any other sort of person in his novel. It was Goncharov's opinion that if an author intended to portray a whole epoch of life, and not only an episode, he was bound to touch upon all the important elements of life. To ignore these elements meant to pull the foundations from beneath the structure and to make everything artificial.

CHAPTER V

Three Thousand Arrests—Vodka Instead of Schools—Official Council—The Magic Circle of Intrigue—War Danger—The Baiting of the Slavophiles—Money for the Bulgarians; None for the Russian Peasant—The Turkish War—The Fatal Mistreatment of a Prisoner—The Fall of Plevna—Disappointed Hopes for a Constitution—The Attempt of Vera Sassulich—A Symptomatic Pardon—The Rage of the Conservatives.

WHEN I returned to St. Petersburg in 1876 I noticed a change in the relationship between Society and the Government. Everywhere, one heard criticism and expressions of dissatisfaction. The Minister of Education, Count Tolstoy and his preference for the classical language aroused the stormy protests of most parents. While they realized the importance of a classical education, they insisted upon a stronger consideration of practical subjects. An open letter from Prince Vassilchikov to Count Tolstoy, printed abroad, was circulated in Society. The writer pointed out the harm of the new educational system and advised the organization of preparatory schools and higher technical institutions. Many other pamphlets of an economic and political nature passed from hand to hand and were animatedly discussed.

One day, I met the famous jurist and philosopher, Kavelin, at the home of the Baroness Rahden. He was in a very pessimistic mood, and complained that talent was dying out among the young people, and was hotly indignant at the limitation of personal liberty and that of the press as well as at the recent numerous arrests. It was just at this time that the famous Shikharov case was drawing to its conclusion. In order to destroy the revolutionary propaganda which had made considerable progress, at one blow, Senator Shikharov had ordered sudden arrests in all parts of the country. It happened very often that perfectly innocent individuals were swept along with the suspects. Of the three thousand accused of the crime, only one hundred and ninety-three were found guilty, after a trial which lasted two years. Those who had not died in prison during that time, or who had not lost their reason, became after their release what they had not been before—rabid revolutionists.

The program of the anti-Government organization consisted in those days of the instigation of anarchy, general destruction and, chiefly, in the expropriation of land. Their means to this end were the distribution of illegal literature and verbal propaganda. With the latter they achieved little success, as the peasants were not yet ready to listen to revolutionary speeches; they drove the agitators away. These conditions showed plainly enough the great mistake our government made in not taking over the leadership of its people by influencing its spirit beneficently by means of education.

The Church, too, could have been of invaluable assistance. But Count Tolstoy, while Minister of Education, held the post of Procurator of the Holy Synod at the same time, and rather tried to condense some parishes into larger units, dissolved others, and in general aimed at reducing the number of religious functionaries to a minimum. He meant by this reform to improve the material conditions of the clergy, as if the Government had not other means of attending to that! Soon the peasants became indifferent to the Church, now that its services had lost so much of their former pomp and ceremony. Instead, vodka began to flow through the villages; for the system of private concessions had been replaced by Government monopoly of vodka.

A noticeable impoverishment of the peasants soon began to show itself. Even during the Valuyev ministry a commission had been formed for the purpose of studying the condition at its source. This commission proved with eloquent figures that the peasants were getting poorer and sooner or later would be reduced to beggary. The awful famine in Samara, which was supposed to remain a secret but which finally could not be denied any longer, proved the correctness of the commission's findings.

What was done to avert the danger which loomed up behind these conditions?

Nothing!

The reports of the commission remained on the council table for several years, until in fact in 1880 another commission, called the Kokhanov Commission, was formed for the same purpose.

How easily the disaster that was later to break over Russia could have then been averted! The revolutionary propaganda as yet had remained without an echo among the people. They were still the chief props of the Monarchy. But nobody cared!

A social and intellectual life was, after all, to be found only in the magic circle of Court and Government. It was here that intrigues, influences, decrees and doubts held their sway, and all these affairs were so foreign to the people's lives and minds, so estranged were they from Sarmatian Russia, that it would seem as if the people and the Government were two different planets. The high officials actually knew nothing about the real Russia.

Threatening clouds appeared on the foreign political horizon. The Southern Slavs had begun to stir. . . .

It is true that there were reasons enough for this, but the unrest was particularly fanned by the agents of our Ambassador in Constantinople, Count Nikolai Pavlovich Ignatiev. The Count was dreaming of a brilliant revenge for the loss of the Crimean War, and thought the time for the fall of the Osman Empire had come. In his imagination, he saw himself tearing down the crescent and raising the cross on the Hagia Sophia.

Committees worked industriously toward this end. . . . Representatives traveled all over Russia and in fiery terms preached a crusade for the liberation of the Slavs oppressed under the yoke of Islam. And, indeed, soon numbers of volunteers poured down the banks of the Danube and offered their swords and their lives for the "holy cause." But who were these people? Most of them were shipwrecked beings, adventurers, sons of landed proprietors who had lost their fortunes in drink and gambling, discharged lieutenants and reserve-officers from the army corps, in short, an undisciplined horde which could easily be won for any chance adventure.

Certainly there were among these also men who had been convinced, who were honestly carried away by Slavophile ideals, and who just as honestly believed that the Russian people had been chosen to defend the cause of all the Slavs throughout the world. Such dreamers were the Kireyevski brothers, who sincerely believed that this artificial movement was the indomitable urge of the Russian people and that the war was a veritable crusade. The younger of these two brothers was a former officer of the Guard, and hastened to be one of the first on the battlefield. He fell in one of the first skirmishes.

Slavophile circles were untiringly active for their cause, and even tried to influence the Empress through her Court ladies. The Countess Antonia Dimitriyevna Bludov, Countess Alexandra Andreyevna Tolstoy and

Ekaterina Fyodorovna Tyutchev, tried their best to persuade the heir apparent to their views, and succeeded in gaining his sympathy. He openly protected the volunteers and permitted the officers stationed in St. Petersburg to join Chernyayev's army in Serbia without losing their military standing in Russia.

The Emperor was abroad during these feverish activities. In the course of a conversation with a group of foreign statesmen, he declared emphatically, that he was against Russian intervention in the Serb-Turkish War. For a while it seemed that this imperial attitude had a quieting effect on the war fever, but it soon became evident that a flame once kindled was difficult to extinguish.

In the Fall came the complete debacle of the Serb troops, and Serbia was threatened with annihilation. It was then that the Emperor stepped in and prevented the otherwise inevitable catastrophe, by proclaiming himself the official guardian of Serbia. Now everybody knew that another war with Turkey could not be avoided.

All this time I had been against this war. But now I realized with sorrow that we were irrevocably drawn into the conflict. I thought we had more than enough to do with our interior problems, particularly that of our peasants. In view of that alone, we should have avoided the war. It was the fate of our poor people to be sent staggering again under the burden of war expenses and sacrifice of life. It seemed to me that with our concern about the Slav-ideal, we were forgetting that we were also Russians. And so I did not share the general war enthusiasm of society.

While I was not surprised at the enthusiasm of the Slavophiles, I could not quite understand why the sober St. Petersburg intelligentsia voted for war. I was to be enlightened presently.

One day, while Nicolai Andreyevich Yermakov called on me, he spoke at some length about the Slav question. When I told him that his interest in this problem surprised me, he answered:

"What do I care about the Slavs? I am thinking only of Russia. Do you really believe that this liberating movement will pass without leaving its trace upon us? Can't you hear our own desperate cry for liberty in it? Do you think that after we have liberated our little brothers in the Balkans, we shall be able to return to the old despotism and outlawry? Impossible!"

His eyes behind his glasses gleamed angrily.

"And if liberty is denied us, it will go badly with sovereigns. Then the personal safety of the Dynasty, of the Emperor himself, will face the danger of—"

He stopped abruptly, rose and left precipitately. His words astounded me. No doubt this was the opinion of his whole circle—the progressive intelligentsia!

Our peasants had always been the object of my interest, and I wondered again and again in those days why our society was so much concerned about the welfare of the Serbs and Bulgarians without a moment's thought for their own peasants. I often suggested that a part of the large sum of money collected for the Balkan Slavs be put to use for our own people, but no one paid any attention to me.

Much of this winter of 1876 was spent with the Countess Volkonski, for we had many interests in common. Among other things, we studied the ancient religions and history together. Elizaveta Gregoryevna had made a Russian translation of a great work by Rawlinson, who had discovered new scientific horizons in Assyrian cuneiform inscriptions. On the evenings which I spent with her, and at which her mother would join us, she read her work to us. The old princess, Maria Alexandrovna, listened with amazement.

"C'est incroyable, cequi intéresse les jeunes femmes d'à présent," she would opine, while she shook her head.

Our most frequent visitor in those days was the Greek Ambassador Braila. He was one of the most eminent, intelligent and cultured professors I have ever met. Greek to the last fibre of his being, he was completely immersed in Plato's philosophy. He often read to us from his own book on this great thinker, which he had written in French. It contained excerpts from the Phaedo and the Republic, besides his own elucidations and commentaries.

In the meantime we were approaching war, step by step. The supplies of the Red Cross were being supplemented and newly furnished. This was managed by the Baroness Rahden and we assisted her. Finally, on April 12th, war was declared by an Imperial Manifesto and our troops were ordered to cross over the border into Turkish territory. Now that the disaster could no longer be averted, it became our duty to suppress all misgivings. Our cue was to keep up the people's courage, and to alleviate as much as possible the unavoidable suffering.

We waited feverishly for news from our army which was crossing the Danube. The crossing was successfully effected but it meant the first serious loss of life. I was just calling on the Princess Eugenia Maximilianovna when the Grand Duchess Alexandra Petrovna entered, bearing a telegram from the Commander-in-Chief, Nicolai Nicolayevich. It contained the message of victory for Russia, and the remark that her son, the future Generalissimo in the World War, had shown great valor.

The Emperor and all the Grand Dukes were at the battlefield. The Grand Duke-Crown Prince commanded the Rustchuck Army. A great many of our acquaintances were among them.

I remember one evening at the home of the Princess Eugenia Maximilianovna—the last one before the departure of her brother Sergei Maximilianovich for the Front. The Prince and I had a long conversation. He was a thorough West European, an artist, elegant and clever. All his sympathies were with Italy, the home of art, science and culture.

"But for these Bulgarians, Serbs and other Slavs," he said to me, "I have not the slightest sympathy."

We decided to go to Hapsal where my mother, as the companion of the Grand Duchess-Crown Princess, had already arrived. The Court had taken the villa of Count Brevern de la Gardie as usual, and our friend Alexandra Alexandrovna Voyeikov had obligingly rented another villa for us. This summer left an indelible impression on me. It was my privilege to be in close proximity to the wife of the Crown Prince, the future Tsarina Maria Fyodorovna, to whom I was deeply devoted. Her kindness, he delicacy, her simplicity and her charming manner, were not new to me, but all these qualities shone still brighter in our intimate association and made me still more appreciative of them.

The progress of the war was naturally our chief subject. Every evening the mail brought the Grand Duchess a letter from her husband at the Front, and she read excerpts from it to us at the tea-table. In this manner, we were able to follow the events, even the small ones, on the Danube. For the rest of the day, we took drives and walks around Hapsal, and I was often chosen to ride alongside the Grand Duchess. Everything would have been perfect had not the thought of the war made us uneasy.

The older generals shook their heads when they heard

of the rapid crossing of the Balkans by our troops. They considered the quick advance with unprotected lines of retreat, very imprudent. In order to avoid this danger, our army made every effort to take the Fort Plevna. But they remained unsuccessful, and the event was costly in the loss of human lives.

The pity which we felt for our soldiers, when we heard of their heroic defense of the Shipka Pass or of their slaughter on the heights of Plevna, turned to hatred for the present Government, which was responsible for all these sacrifices and failures.

The Grand Duchess went to Peterhof to see the Emperor several times. Once on her return from one of these visits, she told us about some dreadful incident in a prison. Indignantly, she related a story about a clash between the Commandant of St. Petersburg, Trepov, and a prisoner by the name of Bogolyubov, which had ended with a bodily chastisement of Bogolyubov. One evening, at the Empress's apartments, this incident was retold. The Grand Duchess-Crown Princess again could not refrain from expressing herself very feelingly about this despicable act of despotism on the part of Trepov. The incident had its consequences; for the Nihilistic propagandists made capital of it. Its fatal result was an attempt on Trepov's life by Vera Sassulich.

After my return to St. Petersburg, I chanced to have a talk with the Governor of Kharkov, Prince Krapotkin. In the course of our conversation, I suggested that one might teach our revolutionists better faith in humanity by the refutation of their unfounded prejudices—and by personal social contact.

"Don't believe that," cried the Prince. "It's an illusion. The people are implacable, and they hate us on principle. Me, because I am a Prince and Governor; you, because you are a great lady. It is a war to the bitter end. We must destroy them, lest they destroy us!"

Poor Krapotkin! A year later, he was murdered by the revolutionists.

St. Petersburg was depressed. It was just after the third battle at Plevna, which had demanded a toll of many lives again, but again had not been successful. All eyes, all thoughts, were turned toward this city—unknown till now, whose hills ran with Russian blood. When finally, on the evening of November 28th, the news of Plevna's fall arrived, the enthusiasm was boundless. All of Russia shouted with joy and breathed with ease once more. Then came the wintry passage across the Balkans, the triumphal march up to the gates of Constantinople, and finally, the sudden standstill, and then—after having undergone superhuman hardships—the feeling of utter weariness.

In the autumn, the Emperor returned to his Capital. He had aged, and his face bore the traces of the nervous strain he had suffered.

All minds seemed to be fermenting with an all-pervading unrest. After her great sacrifices for the liberation of the Bulgarians, Russia felt that its own hour of reward had come, its own liberation from a despotic rule. Everyone spoke openly of the Constitution. This word seemed forever in the air, it stared at one from every newspaper column.

But the tension broke in an entirely unexpected way. The Minister of State, Alexander Yegorevich Timashev, summoned all representatives of the press and announced to the assembled men that there was no intention of giving the people a constitution and that the papers were strictly forbidden to write about it.

Once again a decisive moment for action had been missed.

The Chancellor, Prince Alexander Michailovich Gorchakov, shared my misgivings in regard to the Emperor's course of action. His daughter-in-law, the young princess, nee Sturdza, also agreed with us, and Gorchakov, during a conversation about our internal politics, said to me with a very worried air:

"C'est une question bien plus sérieuse que celle de l'Orient."

Timashev, Minister of the Interior, was completely entangled by a web of court intrigues which blinded him to the realities of the existing conditions. His one object was to extirpate the revolutionary movement by violence. The notorious "Third Division" worked sedulously in that direction. Their leader, Count Peter Andreyevich Shuvalov, attained such power that he was called Peter IV. In the meantime, the condition of the peasants grew increasingly worse, to some extent in consequence of the war. The Valuyev Commission had drawn attention to this but reforms in this field were deferred for the future.

Symptoms of the ominous ferment in all circles became more and more apparent. One significant incident was the famous attempt on the life of Trepov, the Commandant of the City of St. Petersburg, by Vera Sassulich. At one of his customary receptions Trepov was shot a number of times in succession by the young girl who had posted herself quite close to him. He was seriously wounded. At the trial, she deposed that she had no personal grudge against Trepov; that she had intended only to avenge the maltreatment of the prisoner Bogolyubov.

There was no question of its being anything but a political crime. Yet the Minister of Justice, Count Pahlen, who had been the object of numberless accusations in the "Trial of the 193," was anxious to avoid another political case and insisted on trying the Sassulich Case as any ordinary attempt at murder before the jury. The former Attorney General, Anatole Fyodorovich Koni, our good friend, was elected chairman of the Tribunal.

A few days before the hearing of the case, we were all dining with the Grand Duchess Ekaterina Michailovna, and Koni told us some details of the trial which had not been revealed to the general public.

"What worries me is that Count Pahlen has decided to classify this crime as non-political," he said. "I fear it will end with an acquittal."

"Acquittal?" we all cried, astounded. "But isn't this murder?"

"According to the temper of society, I am inclined to think that such a decision is not at all impossible, particularly when the jury will be face to face with and listening to the witness of the mistreatment in prison."

"What? Do you mean to say that these witnesses will be allowed to appear?" asked the Grand Duchess. "That means that not the Sassulich, but Trepov, will be on trial!"

On the day of the trial, the courtroom was filled to overflowing; everyone wanted to be present at this much-discussed case. We watched the defendant with curiosity. She was dressed modestly. Two long, dark braids fell down her shoulders; her manner was simple and natural. When certain questions were put to her, she answered in a lightly tremulous voice:

"It is hard to raise one's hand against a human being, and I have always hoped and waited for the Government to interfere with the evil practices. But time went on, I lived as in a dream, and then I decided. . . . I wish one didn't have to repeat these things over and over again."

Koni tried to be as unbiased as possible in his position as Chairman. I had the impression that he was working toward a sentence with extenuating circumstances. The speech of the Attorney General was exceptionally ineffective. His voice was pitched so low that one could hardly hear him, and he was so excited that he had to resort to repeated sips of water, as if he were about to faint.

The appearance of a number of young political prisoners created quite a stir. They had been brought into the courtroom from the Peter-Paul Fortress, merely as witnesses of the incident in prison. Their pale faces, their voices trembling with tears and indignation, the details of their depositions—all these statements made me lower my eyes in shame. Then the strong, bombastic voice of the attorney for the defense, Alexandrov, rang out. First, he elucidated the depositions, and then he mercilessly disclosed the whole despotism of government power. The public, at the occasion of a particularly effective phrase, broke into endless, violent applause. It was true indeed—on that day it was neither Trepov nor the Sassulich who were being tried, but the administration. And everyone understood the meaning of the manifestation.

The jury pronounced the verdict. It was acquittal. The judge, jury, dignitaries and officials grown grey in the service, the whole public—everyone—was carried away by the mood of the moment. One could not analyze it, but it swept over everyone, without exception, even the soberest of them, in that dramatic moment.

When the Sassulich appeared, the whole street shouted and acclaimed her. A rumor had sprung up to the effect that the Government would re-arrest her, whereupon all her women adherents closed in around her and surrounded her like a wall. She was put into a carriage which however could proceed only very slowly through the masses of people. Suddenly a shot rang out—no one knew who had fired it. The carriage stopped and it was discovered that one of the girls had been slightly wounded. She was carried into the nearest apothecary's shop, and it was assumed that she was the Sassulich. The general attention was concentrated on her. Meanwhile, the real Sassulich girl slipped out of the carriage and disappeared in the crowd. The police searched for her diligently, but they never succeeded in finding her.

Society had been deeply impressed by the Sassulich case. Many regarded and celebrated her as a second Charlotte Corday, and did not see the danger that lurked in the pardoning of a political murderer. Conservative circles, on the other hand, were indignant beyond measure, and their rage turned on Koni. Although such experienced jurists as Chicherin, Dimitriev and Shamshon thoroughly approved of his tactics, the public opinion of the reactionary groups branded him mercilessly, and all those doors which had stood open to him hospitably before, were now suddenly closed.

I own to this day a letter from Anatole Fyodorovich Koni, in which he thanks me for my unchanged attitude toward him. But in those days of his fall from grace, my friends wondered at my tolerance and actually censured me. I was at once accused of dangerous sympathies for the revolutionists. To this day, there are narrow and superficial minds who claim that Koni actually let loose the revolution and that all the later catastrophes would not have happened if Vera Sassulich had not been pardoned.

Tsar Alexander II

The Michael Palace

CHAPTER VI

The Revolutionists' Death Warrant for the Tsar—The First Assault—Timid Reforms—Projects—The Infernal Machine in the Emperor's Palace—Count Louis Melikov, Dictator—The Appointment of Pobyedonostzev as Procurator of the Synod—The Secret Marriage of Alexander II—Court and Family Scandal—The Crown Princess Walks Into a Trap—A Moment of Imperial Wrath—The Last Hours of Alexander II—The Catastrophe—"A Formal Reception" in the Face of Death.

In Taine's beautiful book on revolutionary France, he speaks of Society playing with revolutionary thought as with a young predatory animal, and describes how Society refuses to see the animal gradually mature, grow wild and finally change into a monster. This same process took place in Russia, where the revolutionary movement gained more and more ground. The numbers of arrests began to mount dangerously, and political murders increased. The new Chief of the Third Division, General Mesenzev, was killed in broad daylight, and although the Nihilists had thus far not dared to attack the Imperial Personage, they now decided to change their tactics. In 1879, at the congress of revolutionist leaders in Leipzig, it was decreed to sentence the Emperor Alexander II, the liberator of the serfs, to death! There followed a series of attacks on him.

Social life continued to move in its well-worn grooves. But there was no zest in it. The Empress's health had grown worse, and the Court Balls had to be conducted without her. Turgenyev appeared in St. Petersburg again that winter where, to his surprise, he was loudly acclaimed. His connections with the Russian political emigrants in Paris were well known, and his friendly relationship with Lavrov, their leader, had been particularly noted. So that this festive reception of Turgenyev was in the nature of a demonstration of sympathy, which, on account of the existing censorship, was the only means of its manifesting itself.

I saw him often during this visit to St. Petersburg. He rarely spoke of politics in my presence, but I remember how vexed we were with his bourgeois manner, which had evidently been adopted from the Viardot family. In artistic matters, however, he had preserved all the freshness of his cultured mind, and his conversation was —as before—entrancing.

On April 2nd, the Emperor took his customary morning walk. At the Moika, close to the Singer-Bridge, a young man came up to him. The Emperor's suspicion was aroused immediately. He beckoned to a policeman, but that creature stood at attention, staring at the Emperor with fixed eyes, and did not notice the approaching man, who suddenly shot at the Emperor a number of times, without, however, hitting him. He was arrested, and found to be a certain Solovyev, a member of the revolutionary party.

I spent the following summer at the Baltic; but as soon as I returned to St. Petersburg the atmosphere of danger and the excitement began to weigh heavily upon me. As the Emperor was returning from the Crimea, two other attempts were made on his life, one while he was still in the South, the second near Moscow. A powerful charge of dynamite was laid under the tracks on which the Emperor's train was to pass. A fortunate accident prevented the threatening disaster once again, but the evident determination and malice of the murderers created a general feeling of horror, and dark forebodings depressed all of us.

The Empress was dying in her apartments in the

Winter Palace. Her condition was hopeless, and already everyone was openly discussing the Emperor's relations with the Princess Yuryevskaya. Since Solovyev's attack upon the Tsar, the Princess had taken up her quarters in the Imperial Palace in order to spare the Emperor the necessity of driving to her house. The Tsar had changed noticeably during these months. He seemed restless and irritated, his eyes had lost their customary kind expression and he looked sullen and suspicious.

The numerous arrests, which had become the order of the day, served only as a light covering for the swelling spread of dissatisfaction among the people. It didn't improve conditions in any way. Simultaneously, rumors about the grave misdeeds of the administration had begun to circulate. These rumors were not always groundless. Many fair-minded men realized sadly and helplessly that such a state of affairs was bound to undermine the authority of the Government still further, and to fan the revolutionary propaganda. In a conversation with me, P. P. Semeonov complained:

"We had, and we have, as no other country has," he said, "invaluable means of preventing this menacing revolution. We own a wealth of land, which ought to be preserved for the people, and for the still growing population. Instead, we allow this precious possession to be exploited shamelessly by a few adventurers. The disaster, which must inevitably follow such a system, will be indescribable!"

Semeonov's forebodings became stern realities before our very eyes, only a few decades later.

On January 1, 1880, my old friend Valuyev was appointed chairman of the Cabinet Council. He was worried about the administration, and said to me on one occasion:

"The Government carriage seems to be drawn by

horses which all strain in different directions. They become prostrated by the effort, but the carriage does not move."

Valuyev also tried to submit a project to the Emperor wherein he suggested, among other measures, the convocation of the representatives of all the Provinces to meet in council whenever important matters of State were to be decided. But although Valuyev had the audacity to compose the petition, he lacked the courage to defend it against the aggressions of the Grand Duke Konstantin Nicolayevich. The Grand Duke saw in the proposed measure a hazardous step toward a constitution. And as the Emperor began to share his brother's opinion, Valuyev relinquished his plan at once.

What had the Emperor achieved by the time he reached the end of his twenty-five years of government, the commemoration of which was to be celebrated on February 8th? He was probably the last one to realize that his good intentions had never led to their fulfilment, because no plan had been carried out thoroughly. For this same reason, even the liberation of the serfs remained only half a deed, since no adequate economic organization of the new order had been provided simultaneously with their new freedom.

On February 5th, a family dinner was to be held at the Winter Palace. Prince Alexander of Hessia, the brother of the Empress, was expected, and in consideration of the arrival of his train, the dinner hour had been deferred for thirty minutes. The Crown Prince and the other Grand Dukes had driven to the station to meet the Prince of Hessia. But the Crown Prince's wife arrived in the Winter Palace at the appointed hour. Immediately upon entering she was struck by the darkness and draft within the palace. The Emperor who came forward to greet her, explained, "We just had a powerful gas explosion."

"But," answered the Grand Duchess, "it doesn't smell at all like gas—rather like gunpowder."

The Emperor's remark had indeed been a white lie. A revolutionist had blown up the dining-room in which the whole Imperial family was to have dined, with an infernal machine. Everything had been calculated with fiendish precision, so that the explosion would have happened during the meal. If the arrival of the Prince of Hessia had not necessitated the delay of the dinner, not one of the diners would have escaped death. As it was, the Guard, which was composed almost entirely of members of a Finnish regiment, suffered the greatest loss. A number of soldiers were dead, many were severely wounded.

One can imagine the general excitement! The Emperor hurried to the apartments of the Empress, fearing that the emotional shock might have been too much for her in her precarious condition. But she had heard nothing. A deep sleep drugged her consciousness. Completely undone, the Emperor took a chair and sat down at the door of the Empress's bedroom. With his head buried in his hands, he waited in deep, speechless agony until she woke. He wanted to be the first person to see her, and to be the one to report about the explosion and the miracle of the escape!

The horrible news spread rapidly, and on the following morning a Thanksgiving service was ordered in the Palace, which all of us Court ladies attended. The Emperor himself was a sad and noble figure as he entered. After the service I walked to the Saltykov entrance, hoping to come across the Grand Duchess Maria Alexandrovna. Then I saw myself, the frightful destruction wrought by the bomb, of which nothing had been noticed in the gala rooms. The flagstones were torn up and holes gaped everywhere. In order to penetrate to the apartments of the Grand Duchess one had to work one's way through mountains of rubbish. I sent my name to the Grand Duchess and was received. It was from her that I heard an excited but detailed account of the occurrence on the previous evening.

What would happen next? That was the question everyone was asking. It now began to be rumored that the posts of Governor General were to be abolished, and a Dictator appointed in their stead. I drove to the home of the wife of Governor General Gurko, hoping to hear more. A few official personages were there when I arrived, and Madame Gurko was saying that her husband was leaving his post. A conference with the Emperor had just taken place, and its result was the setting up of a dictatorship, for which Count Loris Melikov had been proposed. The proposal was verified only a few hours later, when the Emperor appointed him.

The police investigation at work on the recent outrage in the Winter Palace resulted in the discovery that its perpetrator was gone. He had evidently managed to reach the nearby Swedish border, and had fled to safety. The police were only able to ascertain that the man was a carpenter who had been employed in the Palace and had been allowed to live in the servants' quarters there. It became known much later that this carpenter was none other than the well-known revolutionist, Kholtunov. Still later he himself admitted and described the deed in a pamphlet, printed abroad.

St. Petersburg continued to be depressed and excited. The Grand Duke Michael, who had just returned with his wife after a long absence in the Caucasus, could not suppress his astonishment at the change that had taken place in the temper and conversation of the people.

"I don't know St. Petersburg any more," he said to me. "It seems like a nightmare to me. I don't believe that I am awake."

Hardly had Loris Melikov assumed his new duties, when an attack was made upon his life. Fortunately, it failed. In those days I often met him at the Countess Levashov's, and had occasion to study his character closely. His Eastern, flexible mind manifested itself in his small, sly eyes. Although he was not equipped with that thorough education which his high office demanded, his quick perceptive powers enabled him to adapt himself to his duties at once. Apparently his manner was frank, but it would have been a mistake to trust his sincerity too far.

He lost no time, but started to work at once, principally on the revision of such documents which referred to the banishment of certain individuals by the administration. This meant the examining of the prisoners, the release of innocent ones, and the proper punishment of the guilty, according to their crimes. The first measures passed by the new Dictator were enthusiastically applauded by the liberal groups and great hopes were set on the new regime.

On February 19th, just two weeks after the explosion, we were all gathered in the Winter Palace to celebrate the twenty-fifth year of the Emperor's reign. The general nervousness had not as yet subsided; some dignitaries had gone so far as to leave St. Petersburg in order to evade being present at the ceremony. Every personal association with the Emperor seemed dangerous in itself.

It goes without saying that everything was done to give the day a festive lustre. After the public audience, the Emperor received the pupils of the military school; in the evening there was a grand illumination, and a gala performance in the theatre. But despite the lavish entertainment, a paralyzing sense of fear and anxiety weighed on the guests.

While the superficial social life took its usual course, the carnival brought its balls, and the inevitable intrigues were spun in official circles, a great political change was in process of preparation. The Secretary of State, Makov, and Count Dimitri Andreyevich Tolstoy were avowed opponents of Loris Melikov, and they often criticized his mistakes which were due to his ignorance of court etiquette, and to his lack of experience in politics. But by means of his craftiness and pliancy, he always succeeded in extricating himself from any situation, which faculty earned for him the name of an unreliable "Jongleur." He had as many enemies in society as he had adherents.

In the end, he succeeded in bringing about Count Tolstoy's dismissal. After long hesitation, the Tsar gave in to this. At Easter time, this decision of the Emperor's was made public, with the simultaneous appointment of Saburov as Minister of Public Education and Pobyedonostzev as Procurator of the Synod. The news of these changes, which was broadcast just on Easter eve, released an outburst of acclamation in St. Petersburg and indeed throughout Russia. Rarely have I seen so unanimous an opinion regarding a political event. Count Tolstoy was deeply wounded by the public's attitude, but was able to taste satisfaction two years later when Alexander III made him Secretary of State.

His successor as Procurator of the Synod, K. P. Pobyedonostzev, seemed to be the right man in the proper place. An enthusiastic son of the Church, a devotee to all its customs and traditions, he seemed almost destined to thoroughly reform and spiritualize our Church.

At this time, the condition of the Empress was rapidly growing worse. Anastasia Nicolayevna Malzev, the sister of Prince Sergei Nicolayevich Urussov, watched at her bedside ceaselessly. She was enthusiastically and jealously devoted to the Empress. According to her story the Empress, shortly before her death, desired to see the Crown Prince alone, and they remained together for a long while.

On May 22nd the Empress died alone and unnoticed. When the Emperor called on her that morning, he found her dead. Shortly before, he had gone to live at Tsarskoye Selo, but now came back to St. Petersburg and the entire family gathered for the usual pompous funeral ceremony.

Loris Melikov enjoyed the unreserved confidence of the Crown Prince at that time, and the latter subscribed to all his measures and relied firmly on his sincere devotion. Melikov's authority grew even greater when he announced to the Emperor that, in his opinion, quiet had become so firmly established again, that there was no longer a necessity for extraordinary measures. In consequence of this declaration, the Supreme Commission was abolished, Loris Melikov resigned from his exalted office with dignity, and accepted the comparatively modest post of Secretary of State. At the same time the notorious "Third Division," which had long excited and irritated the public mind, and which was regarded as the source of all evils, was superficially changed. This department was turned into a "gendarmerie corps" under the jurisdiction of the Ministry of State. Although in reality conditions remained as before, the people approved of this change enthusiastically. Loris himself was eminently satisfied with this measure, and once said: "No matter how I may be judged some day, one thing no one will deny me: the abolition of the 'Third Division.' "

At the end of June, the Grand Duke-Crown Prince and his wife returned from Hapsal to St. Petersburg to attend the mourning service in memory of the late Empress, forty days after her death. In the meantime, the Imperial children remained under the care and supervision of my mother. Shortly after, the Emperor summoned the Crown Prince and told him of his already consummated marriage to the Princess Yuryevskaya. This marriage had been performed in all secrecy on June 6th; not even Loris Melikov knew in whose presence the ceremony had taken place.

The Emperor now explained to his son and the Grand Duchess: "I have done what I was impelled to do by my sense of duty to the Princess and her children. I felt it my duty to clear up her position and that of her children and to ease her conscience of the burden which I had imposed on it. It was impossible to delay another day, for both of you know very well that I am not sure of my life for a single day—that death is hovering over me always. I repeat: this step has been taken chiefly for the satisfaction of my conscience. Everything will remain as before, nothing has changed, and therefore I beg of you not to speak about this to anyone."

The Grand Duke and his wife returned to Hapsal rather depressed, but they guarded the secret. It was only much later that my mother learned all the details from them.

But, as it soon developed, the Princess Yuryevskaya was not satisfied with the modest part which the Emperor had intended for her when he married her. When she arrived in the Crimea in the Emperor's company, she refused to stay—as had been her custom—in her own villa, but insisted upon occupying the apartments in Livadia Castle, which as the legally married wife of the Tsar, she considered it her proper right to claim—that is, the rooms of the late Empress.

Up till then, it had been a tradition in Livadia to assemble the entire Imperial court about the Tsar's table at mealtime; but now the Emperor breakfasted and dined alone with his wife, and a special table was set for the court, the so-called "chamberlain's table."

In the meantime Count Loris Melikov was growing livelier and merrier. He did not hesitate to air his opinion of the Princess Yuryevskaya behind the Tsar's back, and on the other hand he outdid himself in endless favors and flattery and pretended to be one of her most ardent admirers when face-to-face with her. All this, in the hope of gaining the Emperor's confidence, which he needed for the accomplishment of his plans. He even took it upon himself to satisfy the ardent wish of the Yuryevskaya—which was to meet the Crown Princess. This, however, was no easy task, and could only be achieved by means of a ruse, a circumstance which did not deter Melikov for an instant. In this episode the whole duplicity of this Armenian appeared in its full flower, and his act was doubly despicable in face of the kindness which he had experienced at the hands of the Crown Prince and his wife.

Had Loris known that the significance of the Princess Yuryevskaya would amount to nil in less than half a year, he surely would have hesitated, at that time, to forfeit the confidence of the Crown Prince and future Tsar. But he could not know it! . . . In the name of the Emperor he transmitted an invitation to the Crown Prince and his wife to spend the late autumn in Livadia. At first only the Crown Prince meant to go, but Loris insisted especially upon the visit of the Grand Duchess, too. Not once during the conversation did he mention the name of the Princess Yuryevskaya. So that the Crown Prince and his wife had no idea that the Princess was not living in her villa any longer, but in the Emperor's Palace. They accepted the invitation, and it was not until they were on the steamer between Sebastopol and Yalta that Loris mentioned the fact that the Princess was in Yalta and mentioned the position which she now occupied.

In telling me all these details much later, the Grand Duchess cried indignantly:

"Just think of it—he waited until we were on the boat and could not return. Had I known it, while we were still on the train, I could have simply left and taken another back to Hapsal, but here we were—trapped!"

Their yacht was approaching Yalta, and arrived at the appointed hour. The Emperor himself stood on the dock awaiting his children. After the first words of greeting, he said to the Grand Duchess:

"Katharina was unable to come, because she is not quite well; she begs you to excuse her—she will greet you in Livadia."

Not at all embarrassed, the Grand Duchess answered:

"I believe she has done very well not to come. You have impressed me so seriously with the secrecy of the affair that I have obeyed your wish to the letter; no one in my entourage knows anything about it, and the presence of the Princess here would have created surprise and gossip."

The Crown Prince and his wife occupied a special wing of the Castle in Livadia, but came to luncheon and dinner regularly to the main castle, where the table was always set for four people. On Sundays, both couples with their respective entourages would join us at the "Chamberlain's table."

The Crown Princess had summoned my mother to Livadia. As soon as she arrived, the Emperor addressed her and said: "I shall introduce my wife to you today—be good—and kind to her!" He then brought the Princess Yuryevskaya to my mother and introduced her. After dinner, the Emperor joined my mother again and told her in a long conversation how he had met the Princess while she was still a child in the home of her parents in the Government Poltava, and how even then her beauty had fascinated him.

This beauty was still well preserved, and in fact had developed more splendidly. The Princess was not very tall and had a fresh complexion, but she was inclined to fullness, although she was only thirty. Not being endowed with any great intellectual gifts, she was rather ignorant, and had no idea of the manners and customs of high society. Her retired life at the convent school, where the Emperor had already begun to court her, was not likely to have given her a true picture of life in general, and directly upon leaving school she had slipped into this oblique position. It can be readily understood that her constant tactlessness shocked the Court again and again, especially as she took no pains to restrain her temper. She had no self-control, and in her personal quarrels she was rather ordinary. Thus, even ignoring any question of class distinction, the Imperial family had reason enough to look upon her with disfavor and even to bear her a certain secret grudge. The Emperor, on the other hand, passionately desired to bring his second wife into close union with his family. But all his efforts to this end were in vain.

Such was the sultry atmosphere that pervaded the court the following winter, which passed slowly and heavily. Despite the Tsar's efforts at conciliation and his openly displayed annoyance, the two camps drew farther and farther apart. Invitations to family dinners had to be accepted—they were equivalent to orders. Also, such visits as etiquette demanded had to be exchanged; but the Princess was never asked to the soirées which the young members of the Emperor's family held. The Emperor was annoyed; almost angry. These relations led to disagreeable scenes, and increased the Princess's tactlessness; she had by this time become a much-discussed theme in the circles of the Grand Dukes.

The greater the resistance which his family offered the Emperor, the more he tried to exalt the position of his wife. In fact, he toyed with the idea of making her his Empress and having her crowned in the Kremlin. He had already made the initial step toward the realization of this project, by ordering the Act concerning the coronation of Katharina I to be brought to him from the Archives of the Kremlin in order to arrange an analogous ceremony for his wife.

The great Fast Days had come. On Friday night the Imperial Family gathered in the Malachite Hall of the Winter Palace for the purpose of following the traditional custom of asking forgiveness from one another before the evening meal. The year before, the dying Empress had participated in this ceremony. It was therefore natural for her children to remember that hour in a spirit of melancholy. But the Princess Yuryevskaya could not share this mood with them. In an all too sprightly manner, she walked up to the Crown Princess to comply with the formal court etiquette. The Grand Duchess gave her her hand, but did not kiss her, as the Tsar had evidently expected. At this omission the Emperor broke into a torrent of impassioned language, charged with the accumulated wrath of months. He reproached his daughter-in-law with her heartlessness.

"Sasha is a good son," he cried, "but you—you have no heart!"

The assembled court trembled. Not one escaped a scathing remark from the Emperor except the Crown Prince whose correct deportment the Emperor appreciated. The Crown Princess was in tears, and remained far from composed even on the following day. Finally the Emperor approached her and spoke touchingly and cordially to her about the incident on the previous night. He expressed his regret at having grieved her and they were quickly reconciled.

It was on the same day on which he met his violent death that the Emperor ordered Loris Melikov to prepare the rescript of a project for the Imperial signature after it had been submitted to the Government Council. It was an Act which was to give the Provincial Assembly (Zemstvo) a vote in matters of urgent reform.

I remember how indignant I was when, some time later, I happened to read a book by Krapotkin in which he speaks of this Act of Alexander II. He says that the Emperor resorted to this measure only from fear of a new attack upon his person, and Krapotkin regards this as proof of the Emperor's senility and weakness.

Nothing could be more distorted than Krapotkin's interpretation of this act. The Emperor's decision upon this beneficial reform was not due to any revolutionary pressure. It was just at that time that everything was very quiet. Since February 5th of the previous year no attempt had been made to take the life of the Emperor. Besides, the most important of the terrorists had been discovered and Yelyabin, their leader, together with some of his comrades, had been arrested. There remained only to secure one group which centered around Sophia Perovskaya, and even their movements were already being traced. Loris Melikov begged the Emperor to be careful, however, and not to take any drives while this group of conspirators were still at large. At first, the Emperor abided by Melikov's advice. But a parade had been planned at the Michael Manège for March first, and His Majesty expressed his intention to attend. In vain did Loris Melikov implore the Tsar to abstain from this whim; in vain did he even go so far as to seek the intervention of the Princess Yuryevskaya. His Majesty, who had appointed the Grand Duke Dimitri Konstantinovich as personal aide-de-camp for the day, did not wish him to forego this honor, and so insisted upon the drive.

The Countess Antonia Dimitriyevna Bludov was just celebrating her jour-de-fête, and the Emperor stopped to congratulate her. He then drove to the parade and after that, in the company of the Grand Duke Michael Nicolayevich, to the Palais Michael. The Grand Duchess Elena Michailovna told me about this last visit of the Emperor to her palace. She said that His Majesty was perfectly calm, and that he showed no sign of any premonition of his death. He spoke about the children of the Grand Duchess and then the conversation shifted to the topic of free food distribution, which the Grand Duke had organized in his palace. His Majesty asked what sort of people usually came to be fed and if revolutionaries also took advantage of this charity.

Then he rose to go, made his farewells, and stepped out of the house. The Grand Duchess, who had walked with him, remained standing at the door, and continued her conversation with the Grand Duke Michael Nicolayevich.

Suddenly, a frightful detonation shook the building. The Grand Duke rushed out and another explosion followed. The concussion was so powerful that one of the horses, which was just being hitched to the sled of the Grand Duchess, was thrown to the ground. Both the Emperor's feet were blown away. For some strange reason, his uncovered head seemed to worry him most; he groaned and said in a weak voice, "Cold . . ." Count Hendrikov tore off his officer's cap and covered the head of the dying Emperor.

As he was bleeding profusely, it seemed advisable to take him to a hospital, but he clearly and distinctly

Tsarina Maria Alexandrovna with her Grandchild

Tsarina Maria Alexandrovna

ordered them to bring him home. Not for a moment did he lose his will-power or his consciousness.

The Princess Yuryevskaya was awaiting him in the Winter Palace. Before leaving the palace, the Emperor had sent her word to be ready for a drive to the "Summer Garden" with him, directly upon his return. In order not to keep her husband waiting, she stood in readiness for the Emperor, when a valet rushed up to her with the message that the Tsar was ill. She ran down the stairs and met the awful procession. The Emperor was almost lifeless; his blood ran over the floor. . . .

I shall now revert to my personal impression of that woeful day. By sheer accident I had come across the Grand Duchess Ekaterina Michailovna at the end of the services. She told me that she expected the Emperor after the parade. Toward one o'clock, I drove by the Palais Michael, and most likely I passed the murderers in the very act of preparing their evil work. When I arrived at my home, I found the Prince Peter Alexandrovich of Oldenburg, with his tutor, who were making ready to drive with my son and the Grand Duke Nicholas Alexandrovich to the Palais Anichkov. After lunch, the children begged me to play the piano for them, and they began to sing. The noise we made probably prevented us from hearing the explosion. Suddenly the Prince's tutor, who had already left, returned and told us the dreadful news.

I ordered my carriage at once and drove to the Winter Palace. I had to make my way on foot through a surging crowd of people before I reached the door of the Palace. I found it closed and guarded. It was only by way of a detour through the apartments of the Countess Bludov that I was able to penetrate into a corridor close to the Imperial apartments.

Suddenly Bileyev appeared. His face was wet with

tears and, hurrying past us, he cried that the Emperor was dead. We stepped nearer to the door of the death chamber, behind which all the members of the Imperial Family pressed timidly and awe-stricken about the body of the Tsar. All the Ministers of State and the members of the Emperor's suite stood in the corridor; there hung his blood-soaked cloak, and from a side-room they led a wounded Cossack who had just been bandaged. The excitement was indescribable. Everyone expressed a conjecture, told of conspiracies, names were mentioned, uprisings were feared, and the question arose: Have we enough military protection in St. Petersburg?

Suddenly Ivan Michailovich Galitzine appeared and announced in passing:

"Tomorrow we'll have a formal reception."

"Reception?" I asked. "You mean a funeral service."

"No, a ceremonial reception anent the accession to the crown of His Majesty the Emperor Alexander III. Ladies in formal court dress. Gentlemen in gala uniform, but no mourning!"

I shall never forget the "ceremonial reception" on March 2, 1881. When their newly made Majesties appeared, all broke into cries of "Hurrah!" Only a few paces beyond lay the mutilated body of the Tsar, over which the physicians were working in an effort to restore it to something near human semblance, so that it might be shown to the people.

CHAPTER VII

Anxiety About the Coronation of Alexander III—Entry of Their Majesties Into Moscow—Archduke Karl Ludwig of Austria—The Coronation Ceremony—A Banquet in Old-Russian Style—Conversation with the Papal Nuntius—Grande Polonaise in the Kremlin—Prince Alexander of Bulgaria and His Future Successor—The Dedication of the Church of the Saviour—Disappointment After the Holiday Mood.

THE APPOINTED time for the coronation of Alexander III was at hand, and despite the apparent unconcern, a certain feeling of unrest seemed to be in the air, a distressing fear of another murderous attempt. The St. Petersburg police had its eyes sharply on the revolutionists. A group of officers of the guard had made it their personal business to prevent an attack on the Emperor at all costs. Many young people joined this volunteer police organization. While it was gratifying to see their loyalty, they were in no sense an aid to the police.

In view of the enormous mass of people in Moscow,* the police had neither the power nor the ability to prevent an attack upon the new Emperor with any degree of certainty. In the apartment of the Tsar, we all thought with deep anxiety of the long distance the coronation pageant had to cover from the Petrovsk Palace to the Kremlin, all the way through the narrow Tver Street. I was informed that I was to take part in the procession in a carriage, and naturally, the thought of danger to my own person occurred to me. But it was not fear that I felt, but rather pride in the privilege of

*The entire St. Petersburg Court moved to Moscow, the ancient capital, for the coronation which always took place there following an established tradition.

sharing the danger. In order to be prepared for any event, however, I wrote down my wishes and directions in case of any accident to me, which paper I laughingly destroyed after my return from Moscow.

On May 5th, I arrived with the Grand-Ducal couple and their train in Moscow, where apartments had been reserved for us in the Basilevski House in the Vosdvishenkaya Street. The cycle of introductions and visits began almost at once. These visits were very difficult, as we had brought our servants and coachmen from St. Petersburg and they knew nothing about Moscow. Even the street police had been transferred from St. Petersburg and they, too, were unfit to give sufficient local information and directions.

The festivities opened with the entry of their Majesties into Moscow. All the participants were invited to the Petrovski Palace, where I met the Spanish Ambassador and the Duke of Montpernier at luncheon. He was a son of the French King, Louis Napoleon, and the husband of a Spanish Infanta. He was tall and bore a remarkable likeness to the great Henri IV of France; one had only to place an imaginary thick ruff around his neck to complete the resemblance. At the same luncheon I also saw the young and pretty Archduchess Maria Theresia and her husband, the Archduke Karl Ludwig, brother of the Emperor Francis Joseph. She was a Portuguese Princess and much younger than her husband. I was rather annoyed by the Archduke's frivolous manner which contrasted so sharply with my solemnly elated mood.

At the appointed hour the guests rose from the table and went to the Palace entrance. A cannon shot roared, and the Emperor mounted his horse. Behind him rode the Grand Dukes, the foreign Princes, and the train. The Empress took her seat in the gala carriage; after her the Grand Duchesses and the Princesses and then we, the Court ladies, took our places in the gold coaches. As the festive pageant began to move, all participants made the sign of the cross, and it seemed as if a long golden stream were rolling between the file of regiments planted on both sides of the street. Behind the soldiers stood the populace in dense masses, and the roofs were black with people. The shouting increased as we proceeded, the sun shone brilliantly, the bells tolled sonorously. At that moment, no one thought of menacing danger—too beautiful was the scene which recalled Old Russia and the devotion to its Emperor.

The day of the coronation belongs among my most beautiful memories. As Court lady, it was my privilege to view the ceremony from the closest proximity. I could see the pensive face of the Empress distinctly, as she stood in her white dress and her simple coiffure, awaiting the placing of the crown upon her head. The face of the Tsar on that day bore an expression of power and energy, mingled with kindness. That moment when, as the only one in the midst of the standing assemblage, he bent his knee, and with a tremulous voice prayed for God's blessing on his task, made a deep impression on the audience. Presently, he rose with the crown on his head and the scepter in his hand, while all the rest dropped to their knees and joined in the prayer of the Metropolitan.

My neighbor, the Austrian First Lady-in-Waiting, a very distinguished and sympathetic lady, was so charmed with the ceremony that she forgot her fatigue. At the services following the coronation, the Austrian ladies were anxious to have me explain the details of our service to them, so that they were able to coordinate their prayers with ours. I was much pleased with the respect which they as Catholics showed for our sacraments. As we spent a good deal of our time with these ladies during the festivities, we became quite friendly and even the Archduchess began to feel at home in our circle.

On the evening of the Coronation day a gala dinner was given in the Kremlin. The Emperor and Empress sat on the ancient throne-chairs, robed in the ceremonial garments which they had worn in the church. Behind them stood the Grand Dukes and the Princes with their adjutants, and the dishes were served to Their Majesties by the highest Court officials. The Grand Duchesses, according to the ancient custom, were not partaking of the ceremonial dinner, but dined in the "Terema," the women's quarters. The Clergy in their black and white mitres sat on one side of the first table. Opposite them we, the Court ladies, were seated. At the entrance, directly opposite the throne, sat the Diplomatic Corps. The entire ceremony was conducted according to the tradition of the Moscow Tsars. It transported us into that atmosphere and removed us from the forms of modern European life. Even the menu cards were written in old Slavic characters and the dishes were called by Russian names. During dinner, the orchestra played the Coronation Cantata of Tschaikovski and the singer, Madame Lavrovska, performed magnificently. In the evening a gorgeous, festive illumination took place in the city, during which my son and I took a drive. When I finally got home, I was dead-tired and exhausted by this succession of marvellous impressions.

Among the foreign representatives at the Coronation, only the Papal Nuntius had been missing, and he arrived on the following day. As a representative of the Holy See, he could not have attended the ceremonies in the Orthodox Church during the Coronation Day. Monsignore Vannutelli, an extremely clever and cultured prelate, was greeted with an enthusiastic ovation by the

Catholic populace on his drive through the city. We soon found him a socially charming gentleman who fittingly succeeded in combining dignity and graciousness in his manner of the Perfect Prelate. He conversed repeatedly with Pobyedonostzev, and I, too, had several occasions to admire his good sense and the wisdom of his judgments. The Princess Volkonski, who was in high spirits during these dramatic days, was privileged to speak with him oftener than anyone else.

Lisa Volkonski had been carried away by the elated and solemn atmosphere of the Coronation, in addition to her pleasant excitement over Vannutelli's appearance and his social success. He was the very man who would listen to her sympathetically and understand her ideas as no one else could. It had always been her cherished dream to see the Eastern and Western Churches united. She had been brought up in Rome and had a fine understanding of the Catholic Church with its splendid Hierarchy and the rich ramifications of its religious orders which grouped themselves harmoniously, so to speak, about the immovable pillar of the Curia. Her friendship with Vladimir Solovyev only increased her preoccupation with this idea as his "History of Theocracy" had already clearly pointed to the necessity for a spiritual rule of the united Eastern and Western Churches over the civilized world. Solovyev's fancy for Catholicism, however, suffered a severe shock when he visited Rome and became acquainted with the Roman-Jesuitical reality. According to his own words, he came back to Russia more Orthodox than ever.

The Princess Volkonski also discussed this subject with the Metropolitan of Kiev, while in Moscow. The latter was a man of great intelligence and impeccable character, and she was surprised to find him by no means shocked by her theory. According to her idea, the estrangement between the two Churches was simply the result of reciprocal offenses, inflamed through centuries by prejudice and political complications. To destroy these prejudices and to try to arrive at an understanding between Rome and Byzantium seemed to her to be the most important task of our time. It gratified her immensely, therefore, to witness the cordial greetings exchanged by the Metropolitan Platon and the Nuntius Vannutelli, which to her seemed to signify the first step toward the union of the two Churches.

The festivities continued and the day after the Coronation presented another fairylike picture. At the Kremlin, the Grand-Dukes, their trains, and the Ambassadors stepped through the ballrooms to the measures of Glinka's Polonaise from "The Life For The Tsar," between a file of Court ladies, who were dressed in the ancient Russian court dresses. The windows were thrown open on that wonderful warm evening and, looking out, the contours of the cathedrals and campaniles of Moscow seemed studded with myriads of jewels. The Emperor made the first round with the Empress, the next one with the foreign Princesses and with the ladies of the Diplomatic Corps. My partner was Prince Alexander of Battenburg, at that time still the ruler of Bulgaria. He was tall and good-looking, very pleasant and polite, but even upon so short and superficial an acquaintance, he gave evidence of his undeniable snobbery. He boasted that it was he who had suggested advice on the arrangement of this ball to the Tsar, and in speaking of the late Emperor always called him "Mon oncle."

It was there, too, that I met Prince Ferdinand of Coburg, who later succeeded Prince Battenburg as King of Bulgaria. He had been recommended to the Grand Duchess Olga by her older sister, the Duchess of Coburg, and was therefore treated like a member of the family.

I lunched with him in the apartment of the Grand Duchess. He was still very young, and made a rather insignificant impression. He was to prove his political talent somewhat later.

The dedication of the Church of the Saviour formed the apex of the Coronation festivities. The procession all around the Church, with masses of praying people, the singing and the pealing of the bells were particularly splendid and magnificent. My neighbor, the Austrian Countess, was transported by the sight, and repeated every few minutes: 'How sublime!" We never got out of our Court dresses in those days. It was only on the anniversary of the death of the Empress-Mother that the festivities were interrupted. On that day the Imperial family, without their entourage, drove to the Troitsko-Sergeyevskaya Lavra. The military parade on the Khodynski Field formed the conclusion of the grand festivities. There the Emperor received the city elders and delivered his significant program speech.

Thus the Coronation not only had passed without mishap, but it had been carried out with such a display of pomp and splendor that even the foreign guests were kept in a constant state of astonishment. Most of them had expected to find a revolutionary people and an iron police despotism. Instead they were witnesses to a dignified festivity at which the populace had had free access to the Tsar.

Monsignore Vannutelli said to me, as he was leaving: "I was not prepared to see what I have seen. This splendid corroboration of the monarchy is of such magnitude, that I can only compare the Coronation of the Emperor of Russia to the blessing of the Holy Father urbi et orbi from the eminence of St. Peter's dome."

Soon, however, we were to see that these festive days were not analogous to actual conditions and the workdays which followed the holiday brought many and bitter disappointments.

The reform, which had just gotten under way, might have succeeded in taking the wind out of the revolutionary sails, or at least have prevented the influx of new anti-Government elements, if it had been developed in a serious and progressive way. But again the psychological moment was missed. The closest advisors of the Emperor, Pobyedonostzev and Count Tolstoy, did not approve of the new liberal gesture. The Emperor himself, always opposed to compromise, stoutly supported his ministers in enforcing his will by despotic measures rather than through the mediation of public representatives. But at the time, everyone seemed content with the apparently reëstablished order and all anxiety dropped into the background.

CHAPTER VIII

The New Régime—Pobyedonostzev Opposes All Reforms—"The Triumvirate"—The Political Salon of Madame Nelidov—Return to Autocracy—An Ultimatum From the Revolutionists to the Emperor—"Mentir Pasha"—The Pangs of a Prince's Conscience—Politics In Karlsbad—My Mother's Death—Court Intrigues.

But the pressure of fear and anxiety still brooded over the Capital. The very fact that the Imperial couple, at the anxious insistence of Baranov, had stayed away from the mourning services at the Peter-Paul Fortress, created a depressing atmosphere. Every day brought new rumors and surmises and the prevailing tenseness could not be dispelled.

Naturally, the nation was interested what course the new regime would take. We were on the threshold of an era of more acute reaction? At the first meeting of the Cabinet Council, Loris Melikov submitted the project which the late Emperor had signed on the day of his death. The Secretary of War, Milyutin, and the Minister of Finance, Abaza, were both decidedly in favor of Melikov and his proposal, when Pobyedonostzev rose, pale with indignation, and addressed the Council. His voice trembled with agitation as he announced that the submitted program would mean nothing less than a gradual yielding to a Constitution, and that, he added, would signify the collapse of Russia. Pointing to the Peter-Paul Fortress, which one could see from the windows of the Council Hall, he cried that the unburied body of the murdered Emperor was still lying there and that this was hardly the time to reward the revolutionists with dispensations for their benefit.

The Emperor grew pensive under the effect of these words, and decided to postpone his decision. As matters stood, he had no more confidence in Loris Melikov since Melikov had made use of that shameful ruse to trap himself and his wife to please the Princess Yuryevskaya. And so Russia remained in a state of expectant uncertainty.

After the mourning services were over, Alexander III retired with his court to Gachina, which remained his chief residence throughout the years of his reign. In the meantime, the atmosphere in St. Petersburg had by no means cleared up, and when the information spread that a new Crown-Council had been formed, the impatience and curiosity knew no bounds. According to current rumors, the responsible directorate was to be composed of three ministers, and was to be so organized that the dismissal of one of its members would automatically cause the retirement of the two others. Loris Melikov was to be the Chairman. Besides, experts from the provinces were to be called in when the ministry met in council.

The soul and center of all these projects was Elena Nikolayevna Nelidov, at whose home the triumvirate, Melikov, Milyutin and Abaza, often met.

On that evening on which the decision was finally made in Gachina, Melikov, despite his fatigue, hurried straight to Elena Nikolayevna, where he was received like a victor. It had become common knowledge that the Emperor, despite his scruples, had accepted Melikov's project. Melikov was visibly proud of his success, and gladly submitted to having his health drunk in numerous glasses of champagne.

Soon, however, the situation began to change. The Emperor remained suspicious, and thought he had noticed that one of the members of the directorate assumed too much authority. He therefore called Pobyedonostzev to him. The result of this audience was the Manifesto, which was published on April 15, 1881, during the Spring Parade, and which clearly defined the new course. It proclaimed the Emperor's return to the century-old regulations of autocracy. He professed to Orthodoxy and nationalism, and refused to accept any European form of Government, with unmistakable definiteness. All the old traditions were to be re-animated in the spirit of morality, and all education was to be administered by the Church.

The effect of this change of system was staggering. Some believed that this Manifesto, which had been composed behind the back of the Secretary of State, was to show Melikov the Emperor's distrust of him and his policy, and so that, in this way, Melikov might have to resign. Others regarded the Emperor's act as dangerous, while Moscow society—largely conservative—was delighted with this reactionary turn. What could Melikov's Constitution mean to these people to whom traditions were the most important things in life and to whom political progress meant nothing? Had not such innovations already brought Holy Russia to the rim of the abyss?

In those days, there were also many adherents to the side of autocracy, who were honest enough to see the errors of past regimes; but they firmly believed that it was the Emperor alone who could correct the defects of government.

At that time I myself was of the opinion that the Emperor was right in trying to hold the reins of the Government firmly in his hands.

One must remember the Russian situation in those days. Under the then existing conditions, the slightest yielding would have seemed weakness. The Committee of Russian Revolutionists in Geneva had the audacity to send the Emperor a regular ultimatum. In an official note to Alexander III, they declared themselves ready to abandon their terroristic activities if the Government gave the Russian people a Constitution. The Tsar did the only manly thing: he proudly disdained to make a pact with the murderers of his father. And thus he concentrated the hatred of the revolutionists upon himself.

The authority of the Government had been severely shaken, and the most important task of the Emperor was its reëstablishment. The moment seemed particularly favorable, as the tragic end of Alexander II had kindled a sudden spark of patriotism among the people. A general feeling of indignation and hatred toward the Revolutionists, who in their senseless rage had murdered the liberator of the peasants, was rampant. It was, without doubt, the psychological moment to assert the power and authority of the Dynasty.

On the other hand, it would have been wise to have loosened the reins somewhat, as soon as possible, in order to institute certain well-considered reforms at the proper time. This chance was neglected, and constituted the first serious error in the reign of Alexander III.

Count Nicolay Pavlovich Ignatiev, whom the Emperor had known well since the Russo-Turkish War, and whose abilities he had always appreciated, became Secretary of State. It did not disturb the Tsar that Ignatiev's character was not above reproach. His duplicity and craftiness had earned him the name of "Mentir Pasha"* in diplomatic circles. But the Emperor always defended him, explaining that the involved politics of the East necessitated such artifices. He was sure that Ignatiev was honest and straightforward in every other situation. The faith which Alexander III had in his Secretary of State was to be thoroughly shaken.

---

*Sir Liar.

On May 2nd, Prince Peter Georgyevich of Oldenburg died, quite possibly from the effects of the shock sustained in the catastrophe of March 1st when his beloved Emperor was murdered; he had been wholly devoted to Alexander II. The Prince had spent all his life and a great part of his wealth in the services of pedagogy. It was he who had founded our law school, from which so many splendid men were graduated.

Significant of the Prince's nature is the following anecdote which his son, the Prince Alexander Petrovich, told me.

Shortly before his father's death, he found him one day deep in thought. In answer to his son's inquiry, the older Prince said:

"I can't help questioning myself constantly whether I am not partially, if not knowingly, guilty of having helped to bring about the dissatisfaction and hate among the people which culminated in the murder of the Emperor. Have I not, perhaps, often caused indignation and irritation in the course of my activities? My share in causing the disturbances which expressed themselves in that awful deed may be greater than I know."

The Emperor and Empress attended the Prince's funeral, which took place in the Convent Sergeyevski Pustyn. As we were waiting for the train on our way back, the Count Ignatiev joined me and began talking about public opinion. I warned him not to rely on the sympathies of "Salons" alone, and not to neglect the opinions of the people, which habit I believed had been the chief evil of the former system. When I questioned him on his political plans, he answered laconically: "The Assembly of the Zemstvo." (The Provincial Assembly.) But to prepare and organize them would first require a convention of their representatives from the provinces.

A short while later I suddenly became affected by a violent attack of liver complaint and was forced to leave for Karlsbad at once. The trip gave me the opportunity again to compare our miserable, gray villages with the clean, bright settlements outside the Russian border. We arrived at Dresden without stopping, and here the art galleries and particularly the Sistine Madonna delighted me.

After this short rest, Karlsbad and its political circle absorbed all my attention. Several of our highest officers of State were spending their vacations there. I spoke with Count Shuvalov, our Ambassador to London, with Abaza, with H. N. Nelidov and with A. A. Polovzev.

Among the foreign dignitaries at Karlsbad were the German Ambassador to St. Petersburg, General Von Schweinitz, whose viewpoints with regard to the Russian political situation were naturally of great interest to me. The centre of our social life there was the Countess Toll, whom I had met in Oranienbaum years before, when she was still Helene Strandmann. I had not seen her since. She had fully preserved her beauty and youthfulness, and the two daughters in whose company she was constantly to be seen, were no less attractive. One of the girls later became the wife of Isvolski, the Secretary of Foreign Affairs. These three elegant women, always dressed in black, and wearing large black hats, attracted considerable attention on the promenade and in other public places.

I was greatly annoyed in those days by a journalist, a correspondent of the "Chas," who had wheedled his way into the Countess Toll's circle. He made every effort to draw me out on the subject of the relationship between Loris Melikov and Elena Nicolayevna Nelidov, and was specially anxious to get details about the famous cele-

S. Turgenyev

V. Solovyov

F. M. Dostoyevsky

Count A. K. Tolstoy

bration held in honor of "the Dictator" at Madame Nelidov's home. I had great difficulty in convincing him that I knew nothing definite about it. Elena Nicolayevna herself was quite upset about it, and volunteered to give me all the details of that evening with Melikov. As she was fundamentally devoted to the Emperor, she was grieved to see that the situation was made to look as if she had taken Melikov's side against the Tsar. She also persisted in declaring that no champagne had been drunk in honor of Melikov that night and begged me fervently to present the incident—whenever necessary—in a light favorable to her. I placated her with the assurance that it was not my intention to spread rumors about happenings to which I had not been a personal witness.

I left Karlsbad to take the necessary after-cure in Schandau, and from there returned to St. Petersburg. I found my mother not very well. She had aged suddenly, and complained of a feeling of lassitude and shortness of breath. She decided that the Court service was beginning to be too much for her. The new Emperor would want new attendants, anyhow, and so she would retire into private life.

Soon after my return, she went to her beloved Nadeshdino, where she remained till the end of the autumn. Then she returned to St. Petersburg, expecting to move to Gachina later on. A severe attack of weakness incapacitated her, however, and we saw that the end was near. She passed away on November 11th.

The high social position my mother had commanded explained the fact that her death became the subject of conversation for days in St. Petersburg. The Emperor and the Empress called on us immediately, and when I thanked them for their kindness, the Emperor said: "It would have been impossible for me not to have come! Your mother was my teacher and my educator, and her person is intimately associated with the memories of my happiest days."

The Empress wept bitterly at my mother's bier, and repeated that she had loved her like a mother. The funeral was very impressive. The Church of St. Panteleimon was crowded with mourners. While my brothers and sisters accompanied the body to Stepanovski, I remained in St. Petersburg in deep mourning and desolation.

Soon it became unmistakably evident that intrigues against me were being set to work in several social circles. Our intimate relationship with the Imperial family had been an invariable source of envy among some members of our set. While my mother was alive, no one would have dared to express himself overtly on this subject. But now, some personages felt that the time had come to oust me from my position at Court.

A pretext was easily found in the circle of friends which during the winter gathered around the Countess Levashov and myself. This purely intellectual group used to read aloud clippings from the West European newspapers, and this simple fact sufficed my enemies as the basis for a political accusation, which they carried to Gachina, the temporary residence of the Emperor. They claimed that I, together with my "accomplices," was working out a Constitution. In order to appreciate the weight of this charge, one must realize what loathing the very word "constitution" aroused in those days of absolute monarchism.

The Emperor who was told of the rumor actually ordered a secret investigation, the result of which fortunately disclosed the harmlessness of our literary-political activities, and so my enemies could do nothing in the meantime but wait for a better occasion to destroy me.

CHAPTER IX

An Offer From the Grand Duchess Olga Fyodorovna—I Enter the Court Service—Old and New Acquaintances—The Empress Receives—Back in Oranienbaum—An Important Political Event—A Fatal Indiscretion—The Triumph of Count Tolstoy—The End of "Mentir Pasha"—The Cares of a First Lady-in-Waiting—A Winter of Festivities.

IN THE spring, just as I had made all my preparations to move to Stepanovski, my uncle, Prince Boris Fyodorovich Galitzine, suddenly appeared at my house as the bearer of a proposal from the Grand Duchess Olga Fyodorovna, to accept the post of her First Lady-in-Waiting. The Empress had already given her approval.

I accepted the honorary offer after brief consideration, and wrote the Grand Duchess of my acceptance. She answered by inviting me to Michailovsk, where I was most charmingly received. When I drew her attention to the fact that my duties to my family left very little time for service to her, she said cordially:

"I would never have dared to offer you this post, if I could not let you dispose of your time as you pleased. I wish to make no changes in your life. I am merely looking forward with pleasure to a more frequent association with you."

I thanked the Grand Duchess, and could do no less than declare myself satisfied with her arrangements. At that moment the Grand Duke Michael Nicolayevitch entered and asked merrily: "We may congratulate ourselves, may we not? You and my wife have agreed on everything?"

I answered that it was I who deserved to be congratulated, and in this informal manner, my real court service began, and lasted till 1917.

On July 11, 1882, by all highest order, I was formally named First Lady-in-Waiting to the Grand Duchess and received notice to move to Michailovsk. Together with the Princess Kochubi, who had just been named First Lady-in-Waiting to Her Majesty, I was given beautiful apartments in the building of the Imperial Suite. One room of our apartment was a great round salon, with a flower-bordered balcony from which one had a magnificent view of the sea, St. Petersburg and Kronstadt.

At breakfast and at noontime we were together with our august hosts, and there I presently met the six young Grand Duchesses, whom I liked so well on account of their merriment and good spirits. The Court Chamberlain was my old friend Alexey Fyodorovich Tolstoy with whom, years ago, we had acted at our amateur performance, and who used to call on us often before he left for the Caucasus. The Court Lady Alexandra Sergeyevna Oserov, an unusually intelligent and cultured lady, and I became devoted friends, and remained such until her death many years later.

On the lovely summer days of that year, the Empress always received on the Alexander Terrace, where she would recline on a chaise longue, usually dressed in a white negligêe trimmed with white lace. The Emperor often joined us.

In the course of the following months I had occasion to see other residences of the Imperial Family, and for the first time since my girlhood I saw Oranienbaum again. There, all the old memories of my youth returned to me, particularly the picture of my mother which was still so vivid in my heart.

About that time, a political event of far-reaching im-

Princess Maria Fyodorovna Baryatinsky

Grand Duchess Maria Alexandrovna

portance took place. Count Ignatiev was dismissed and was replaced by Count Dimitri Alexandrovich Tolstoy, the former Minister of Education under Alexander II. In a Slavophilic spirit, Ignatiev had tried to create a Provincial Assembly composed of all classes of people, which was merely to have a voice in the council and be of assistance to the Tsar. His formula was something like this: The people shall make suggestions and give counsel, and the Emperor shall rule.

When the Secretary of State submitted this project to the Emperor, Alexander III replied that such reforms were too far-reaching and might easily lead to a constitution. Thus Ignatiev's plans were summarily refused. But shortly before proposing them to the Emperor, Ignatiev had spoken of his ideas to the famous publicist Kattkov, who forthwith published an editorial in the "Moskovska Vyedomosti" in which he discussed every detail of Ignatiev's plan.

Whether this editorial was inspired by the Count and printed in order to better convince the Emperor, or whether it was simply an indiscretion of Kattkov's—at any rate the Emperor was extremely annoyed. He saw in this high-handed dealing one of "Mentir Pasha's" crooked moves, and drew all sorts of conclusions from this suspicion. When Count Ignatiev appeared for another audience with the Tsar, he was told that he had been dismissed from his office, and that Count Tolstoy would be his successor.

This recall into the Ministry signified a great triumph for Count Tolstoy. Since his dismissal as Minister of Education he had lived in the closest retirement on his estate near Ryasan and, forgotten by all, he was forced to bear the greatest unpopularity ever experienced by a politician. Although he had remained silent through all of it, his vanity and his burning egotism had been deeply wounded by his compulsory retirement from political life. And now he had been appointed to the highest post the Empire had to offer! One can imagine his feeling of satisfaction as he accepted the office of Minister of State.

An adherent of the Right Party by innermost conviction, he had always been the avowed foe of any progressive reform, in which reactionary attitude he was strengthened by the catastrophe of March 1st and by his own humiliation at the time.

After leaving the Government service, Count Ignatiev regrettably retired from all public activities. In the right place, his evident diplomatic talents should still have served the country well on many occasions. But he preferred to withdraw from political life, and was content with the chairmanships of a number of humanitarian societies, to which he devoted himself up to the time of his death, twenty-five years later. But despite his retirement the Slavophiles did not forget him, and on the day of the Peace of San Stefano an ovation and other expressions of gratitude were rendered him annually.

November 14th was the Empress's birthday, and after some weeks in the country and in Moscow, I spent that day in Gachina. In keeping with Court etiquette, on gala days one had to appear *en grande toilette* all day, even in the forenoon, and so I left my apartments that morning to present myself in Gachina, resplendent in the fire of my diamonds. A magnificent church service was held first, and this was followed by an endless congratulatory reception which lasted beyond all reasonable length of time, and it was late before we could sit down to luncheon. A grand ball in the evening brought an end to the festal day, which had proved more ceremonious than entertaining.

My official duties kept me very busy that winter. Regimental festivities alternated with receptions and drives, and the preparation for each event gave me a great deal of trouble. Every Saturday I had to compile a list of the names of such ladies as wished to be received by the Grand Duchess, and then I had to ascertain if they really had a claim to that distinction. Our Sundays were taken up by numerous visits, and it was my task to see to it that everything was carried out with the proper ceremony.

The Grand Duchess Olga Fyodorovna was an unusually clever woman, with a sharp critical sense. In some circles she was rather dreaded for her malicious but striking and pertinent remarks. I personally experienced only kind attentions and consideration from her in my nine years of attachment to her suite. But our temperaments were too different to allow any close approach to each other. Her interests centered in social events exclusively, which she followed closely and judged critically. Her striking mode of expression often aroused my risibilities, and to this day I remember some of the clever things she said.

The winter season of 1882-83 was exceptionally brilliant. On November 26th the Imperial Court moved from Gachina back to the Winter Palace in St. Petersburg. One of the opening functions was a grand reception and, following it, a dinner in honor of the Knights of St. George. It was the first time that I was privileged to take part in the Imperial Polonaise, that is, I was included in the stately march with which the members of the Imperial Court opened the ball.

The young Empress was radiant in her rose-colored tulle dress and her diamonds. The Grand Duchess Katharina Michailovna asked me to keep her company in the Malachite Salon. We sat down at a table, and from time to time several members of the Imperial Family sat down with us, so that the conversation touched upon many different subjects.

Supper was served in a hall sumptuously decorated and set out with palms. Everyone was in the best of spirits and the charming gowns of the ladies were admired. The Grand Duchess Maria Pavlovna, who was an enthusiastic and graceful dancer, enjoyed this evening particularly.

The costume ball given by the Grand Duke Vladimir Alexandrovich was, if possible, still more brilliant. Only authentic costumes were worn, and preparations for this affair were begun weeks beforehand. The cloth manufacturer, Saposhnikov, had difficulties in filling all the orders for the costumes of the various guests; for it meant the weaving of costly brocades from which the old Russian Boyar costumes were to be made for the ladies and gentlemen. That evening transported all the participants in the festival back to the days of their ancestors, and everyone regretted the advent of morning which ushered in the sober present-day again, as all the magnificent old-fashioned clothes went back into their presses.

CHAPTER X

The Grand Duke Nicolai Konstantinovich Is Accused of Revolutionary Activities—Phantasies—A Bad Omen and Its Realization—Anxieties and Difficulties—The Emperor and His Young Friends—The Emperor Appoints Me Chairman of the Prison Committee—My "Talent" for Organization—Visits to the Prisons—The Death of Baroness Rahden.

WHILE I was living in Moscow, my daughter and her governess had remained with the Countess Levashov at the latter's estate in Ossipovka. Feeling the need of rest, I joined them there and we all journeyed thence to our estate in Finland where shortly afterward my cousin Genadiev, accompanied by Baron Haller, the Bavarian Ambassador, also arrived. We made several excursions, and once went to see the beautiful Imatra Falls which, in the midst of their surroundings of dark, melancholy forests, belong to the rare sights of Finland.

I often drove to Michailovsk from our estate, and there I happened to meet the Grand Duchess Alexandra Yosefovna, who was at that time very agitated about some news she had of her son, the Grand Duke Nicolai Konstantinovich, who was building extensive irrigation plants in Turkestan at his own expense. He had hired some Ural-Cossacks for this purpose, and at once his enemies in St. Petersburg spread the rumor that the Grand Duke was actually collecting a small but utterly devoted military force with whose aid he was preparing a revolution.

One fact which specially seemed to incriminate the Prince was that he had distributed a picture of himself, signed by his own hand, to each Cossack, and that he was referred to in Turkestan simply as "the Prince." I did my best to dispel the anxiety of the Grand Duchess Alexandra Yosefovna by reminding her that her son had been the recipient of all forms of homage from his earliest childhood, and that this distribution of his portrait to the Cossacks could not signify anything serious.

On the other hand, however, it was not unknown to me that the revolutionists had made several attempts to capitalize the banishment of the Grand Duke for their own purposes; for it was rumored among the "Intelligentsia" that the Grand Duke was the only member of the Imperial family who was earnestly engaged in social studies and research, and that it was this very preoccupation which had led to his banishment. Again, the Grand Duke's opponents reminded every one of the fact that Pugachev's rebellion had been assisted in by these same Ural Cossacks. They added that Pugachev was a favorite subject in the Grand Duke's surroundings.

Still more fantastic were the fairy tales making the rounds in the same circles, to the effect that the Grand Duke Nicolai Konstantinovich was none other than the rightful successor to the throne.

It was only natural that the Grand Duchess Alexandra Yosefovna was worried by all these rumors, especially since Count Tolstoy had explained to her that her banished son did not stand in a very favorable position just at that time.

In the autumn of that year I left for Stepanovski with my daughter, while my husband and our son remained at St. Petersburg. Kira had just celebrated his fifteenth birthday and was to enter law school, so that he was in a way just beginning a new chapter in his life. I was naturally somewhat restless and excited about this, and anxious that we return to St. Petersburg, which we did.

As we were leaving Stepanovski our carriage lost a wheel, which caused the steward to mutter something about a "bad omen," and although I was loath to share his superstitious feeling, still I became increasingly nervous, and dreaded some unpleasant surprise which might be awaiting us when we arrived at St. Petersburg.

I heaved a sigh of relief when I found my son well and content with his new environment. The next day, when I appeared at the Winter Palace for luncheon, the Grand Duchess Alexandra Yosefovna said to me: "I love your face today. It reflects the peace of your soul."

And yet the evil omen did not lie! On the following morning I found my husband dead in his bed. Still and unnoticed, he had passed away in his sleep, after he had spoken to me, late the night before, about Kira's progress in school.

It is impossible to describe the state of mind in which I lived during the weeks and months that followed. . . . It was almost fortunate that just then material worries of a kind I had never known before, broke over me, so that I was forced to take notice of the events of the external world, and thus tear myself out of the depths of my sorrow. Helplessly, I faced a veritable maze of accounts, legal inquiries, denials, dunning letters and documents, and to crown all, two of our stewards had died, one right after the other, leaving debts and hopelessly tangled affairs behind them.

For a while I seriously thought of leaving everything to bury myself in the country and devote the rest of my life to the upbringing of my children. But I realized that I had no right to endanger their careers, and so decided to change nothing in my external life. This decision was made much easier for me by the sympathy and eager help of my friends.

The Grand Duchess had absolved me of all court

duties for the rest of the winter, and my friend Alexandra Sergeyevna Osserov took my place in the interim. The Grand Duchess and her husband both showed me the greatest consideration at every possible occasion; their kindness to me was boundless.

When the Grand Duke Konstantin Konstantinovich married in 1884, I considered it my duty to be present at the ceremony, and thus I appeared at Court again for the first time since my deep sorrow, although inwardly I felt a great reluctance to re-enter society. . . .

On May 6th, the declaration of the maturity of the Crown Prince was celebrated, and this event brought me out of my retirement once again. It was on this occasion that I made the acquaintance of the future German Emperor, Wilhelm II, who had come to St. Petersburg as the representative of his grandfather.

It was a source of great satisfaction to me to find that during the months which followed, my Kira was invited to Gachina time and time again, and several times was asked to remain overnight. It was not only because the bracing air agreed splendidly with the boy, but also because these invitations aided his progress at school. To see an obscure law student appear in the midst of the young Grand Dukes created no little attention. Presently all the military officers became interested in Kira, and the State officials, whose sons were Kira's colleagues at law school, suddenly began to make interested inquiries about my son. The lads were surprised that Kira had never told them of his visits to Gachina, and this modest reticence of my boy's caused him to be generally admired, and spoke well for him.

Often, when the boys were visiting at Gachina they were permitted to join the Emperor on his walks, and he would laugh and romp with them and tease them, just as a father would his children. They would have their

Alexander II with his son, the Crown Prince, his daughter-in-law, and their small son, the Grand Duke Nicolai, who later became Tsar Nicolai II

Alexander II with his morganatic wife and their children

dinner with the Crown Prince in the Palace at noon, and then a special train would carry the young guests back to St. Petersburg in the evening.

As usual, we spent the Summer in the country, and that Autumn moved back again to St. Petersburg. We had hardly settled down, when the Princess Eugenia Maximilianovna asked me to call on her. She had been the Chairman of the Ladies' Committee for Prison Care for the last fifteen years, and it had taken up the greater part of her time and attention. Lately, however, the Government had considerably curtailed the Committee's authority, and so the Princess had decided to resign from her office. She begged me to become her successor.

My own anxieties were weighing so heavily upon me just then, that my first answer was a refusal, although I assured the Princess that I was ready to assist her and to relieve her of some of the work. Fancy my surprise, therefore, when shortly after our conversation, I received a note from her, addressing me as "My dear Madame President." I went to see her immediately, and she showed me a letter from the Emperor in which he thanked her for the work she had done in the past fifteen years, and in which he named me her successor.

In view of this fact, what else could I do but accept the Tsar's appointment! My first step was to become acquainted with the duties of my new office. The Prison Administration immediately showed itself to be co-operative, and both Michael Nicolayevich Galkin and Inspector Zemchevski offered me their help.

But from the very beginning, I found myself in a difficult situation. The Committee of which I had become Chairman was dissatisfied with the restrictions which the Government had imposed on its sphere of activity, and they tried to induce me to make an official protest. Such a step, however, would have made the worst possible impression upon the authorities and the Court, and it was my object to refrain from any such faux pas lest I lose all their good will, and harm the institution which I represented.

There was only one point which I was forced to oppose—I could not tolerate the new restriction which forbade members of the Committee to visit the prisons. And how could our activities result in any appreciable benefits if we did not know how the prisoners lived? I therefore employed all my powers of persuasion to convince the Administration that the activities of the Committee referred to conditions *inside* the prisons and that there would be no point in their beginning after the prisoners had been dismissed. I really succeeded in convincing them of the validity of my standpoint, and from that time on, all our ladies received passes entitling them to regular visits to the prisons.

Despite my honest efforts, it soon became evident that some members of the Committee were not pleased with my activities. Every once in a while they went so far as to complain to the Princess Eugenia Maximilianovna about me, and some of them even tried desperately to undo the relationship which existed between the Princess and myself. I regret to say that these intrigues did not remain without their effect, but happily they never harmed our friendship.

I met Tolstoy, the Secretary of State, at a Court ball, and he greeted me with the words: "Do you know that you are one of my subordinates?" I answered that I knew it very well and that I was proud of it. "And I am very proud of my efficient subordinate," he replied with a smile. "Where in the world did you get that talent for organization?"

It was soon to be proved to me that this remark was not merely a polite phrase, but Count Tolstoy's genuine opinion, for the Count had actually reported my "talent" to the Emperor, with the immediate and gratifying result that all my petitions—and I was not sparing of them—were accepted without question; not one of the cabinet members denied me his signature, and I was also always sure of approbation from the All Highest. It was only natural that I exploited the position which I had thus secured, to the utmost, for the benefit of all the sufferers and those in need of help.

My frequent visits to the prisons gave me a chance to talk to the prisoners and to listen again to the old, yet eternally new, tale of guilt and grief. The multiplicity of human suffering struck me forcibly and, as I myself was no novice to pain and sorrow, I sometimes succeeded in gaining a prisoner's confidence and in imparting to him some words of encouragement. In so doing, I realized the truth of the old saying that the assuagement of others' suffering makes one forget one's own.

My days were so crowded with the prison work and my children's bringing up, that scarcely any time remained for my social duties. It was only on Saturdays that I received, as I had always done, and I can boast that all of St. Petersburg's best society was to be found at my receptions. Occasionally I would have to put in an appearance at a court ball, and now and then I would treat myself to one of the Symphony concerts given in the Hall of the Palace of the Nobility Assembly. There, sitting in the shadow of the Imperial box, I would drink in the strains which brought such balm to my nerves. Sometimes, too, I enjoyed the splendid concerts which were given in the home of the Grand Duchess Katharina Michailovna.

During the winter of 1885, I often met my old friend the Baroness Rahden who, it seemed to me, was beginning to look tired and sad. She was an indefatigable worker for the charitable institutions which the Empress had befriended, and tried unceasingly to urge her august patroness to greater donations and further recommendations, by her moving reports of the misery which she had witnessed. In the course of these efforts she almost invariably met with an obstacle in the shape of Konstantin Karlovich Grot, the Business Manager of these institutions. This fact, together with protracted worry about her sister who was living in reduced circumstances, had their combined effect on the mind of the Baroness, and in addition to her mental state, her depression was further increased by the fact that she had developed cancer. The physicians had advised an operation as being absolutely necessary, a fact which the Baroness kept secret, not indicating by the slightest change in her outward mode of life, what she knew and how she was suffering.

One evening when I went to call on her, together with the Princess Volkonski, I was struck by the unusually affectionate tone of her greeting when we arrived, and by her even more tender farewells. One can imagine our astonishment when we learned next day that she had undergone the dangerous operation.

The operation was successful and the Baroness was able to go abroad once more that Spring. But she was marked by death and she knew it. When she returned to St. Petersburg again in the Fall, she became ill once more, this time hopelessly. In September I called on her, but was not admitted; no one but the nurses could see her. She died on October 9th, and thus again I had lost forever a being who had been dear to me.

Prince Alexander Michailovich Gorchakov

Count Loris Melikov, the Dictator under Alexander II

CHAPTER XI

Johann Strauss In St. Petersburg—The Miracle Worker Johann of Kronstadt—A Ducal Invitation—I Am Accused of Ambitious Intrigues—An Anonymous Letter—An Audience With the Empress—A Family Breakfast In the Imperial Palace—Summer Fêtes In Peterhof—Conversation With the Archbishop Antonin—The Problem of the Sects—Rome's Hopes.

THE FIRST few months of 1886 were so hectically crowded with visits, work and drives, that I became seriously ill, and the doctor threatened that I would not live to see my sixtieth birthday if I continued to live as I had been doing. His prophecy proved wrong! For although I continued to live at a lively pace, I did so for quite a while, and had many an unexpected experience.

In the Spring, the Red Cross Society decided to give a number of concerts for the benefit of their nurseries, and the management was given to me. As a drawing-card for the public of the capital, we decided to invite Johann Strauss to St. Petersburg, for the concerts.

One can't imagine the amount of effort and energy that went into the carrying out of all details. In the end, the concerts proved a success. They took place throughout Easter Week on the Boulevard of the Guarde des Chevaliers, and were attended by the Imperial Family and the leaders of society, in consequence of which we were able to boast of considerable receipts.

My activities during that short concert season had been a veritable ordeal for me, for just at that time my daughter had fallen ill of typhus and I had to hurry to the concert hall from her bedside; as the person actually responsible for the concerts, I had to show myself for a short while at least, and could not stay away from the performances entirely.

In addition to my anxiety over my daughter's health, I was considerably worried about the progress of my son, whose school work had been so splendid at first but which he was now beginning to neglect. The atmosphere surrounding him at law school was so completely different from his home environment, that I often wondered whether the principles of my bringing-up could prevail over these new influences. All this troubled and depressed me mentally as well as physically.

Then it happened that one of my friends advised me to see the famous Father Johann of Kronstadt; he would surely know how to console and comfort me. I became interested, and my friend promised to speak to the godly man about me.

And indeed, a few days later, just as I was preparing to go out for a drive, the visit of the priest was announced. I hurried to the reception room and faced Father Johann. There he stood in the middle of the room in his bright-blue priestly garments with the sun pouring down on him. His clear blue eyes turned to me and he greeted me with a kindly smile. He said that he had just been with the Grand Duchess Alexandra Yosefovna and had come directly from her to me.

I took him into my study and there told him of my daughter's illness, of my anxiety about Kira, and all that had oppressed my soul. He asked me to pray with him, and then spoke to me for a long while in fiery, convincing words. He had a consolation for each of my troubles, and succeeded in imbuing me with such faith in God that I no longer despaired but looked forward to the future with faithful trust.

My health, however, did not seem to improve, and physically I was very miserable. One day while the

Grand Duke Michael Nicolayevich was visiting me, he advised me with kindly sympathy to withdraw to the country completely. The best thing for me, he suggested, would be to come to Michailovsk, where I could not only have every possible comfort, but also the advice of the personal physician to the Ducal couple.

I accepted this generous invitation gratefully, and after placing Kira in care of his guardian, a Mr. von Rehbinder, I moved to the splendid estate of the Grand Duke, which I remembered very well from my first visit there, and took my daughter with me.

The Grand Duke received me himself, and attended to every detail for my comfort, to the very flowers on my balcony. The Grand Duchess expressly reminded me of the fact that I was not to consider myself in office, but to use this time exclusively for the purpose of recuperation.

Accordingly, I had most of my meals in my salon and, with the exception of a few invitations, I was master of my time. I took wonderful daily walks with my daughter through the magnificent park, and we sometime roamed along the shore of the beautiful bay. Occasionally we would drive to St. Petersburg to listen to some specially fine concert. On one of these trips I met the Prince Ivan Michailovich Galitzine. He seemed stunned at the sight of me and greeted me by almost shouting the question: "You are in St. Petersburg, Madame?" I did not understand why this simple fact should have so astonished the Prince; but I soon learned the reason.

Shortly after this meeting in St. Petersburg, while I was lunching with the Grand Duchess, the conversation turned to the subject of personal ambition, and the Grand Duchess asked me whether I was not ambitious. Upon my denial, the Court Steward, Emanuel Sergeyevich Muchanov, who was at table with us, cried in astonishment: "What? And all St. Petersburg is talking of nothing else but your material ambition."

"My ambition!" I asked, completely taken aback.

"I should say. The Princess Kochubi received an anonymous letter just recently, which told of your personal ambition to remove her from her office and to play the first rôle at the Imperial Palace yourself. Your recent presence in St. Petersburg has corroborated that impression."

One can imagine how crushed I was by these calumnies. I dreaded to think that my hostess believed these accusations, and that she was perhaps under the impression that I had used her hospitality for my own ends.

I did not know how to defend myself. The Grand Duchess regarded me expectantly, but I thought I saw at the same moment that she realized my sincerity. Yet there is no doubt in my mind that up to that hour she must have had some doubts as to my motives. I later discovered that she had made some inquiries about my character of Alexandra Sergeyevna Oserov.

I was completely in the dark as to the source of the anonymous letter received by the Princess Kochubi. That this letter actually existed, and that it had had the desired effect upon the Princess, was true beyond a doubt, as she had shown the missive to her niece, the Princess Volkonski, and also to the Princess Wittgenstein, and had asked both whether they considered me greedy for office.

It was clear to me that this despicable trick had had its origin in an atmosphere of envy, and as I knew how difficult it invariably is to refute these calumnies spread in Court circles, I feared that the Empress herself might get a mistaken impression of me. As Her Majesty's good will meant very much to me, I became anxious about my position at court.

It happened that I had a report to make to the Empress on some business connected with her charities, and I asked for an audience. Under the circumstances, I experienced a feeling of great satisfaction when a telegram notified me that the Empress was ready to receive me. At least I would have the opportunity to study the mood at Court.

I was somewhat agitated when I drove to Gachina at the appointed time. There I was met by the Princess Kochubi, First Lady-in-Waiting to the Empress. Her greeting was very cool as she conducted me to the Tsarina, who received me most graciously. She heard my report, and then said to me: "You will lunch with us—in the meantime, please wait for just a few minutes."

I found the Grand Duke Michael Nickolayevich and his wife in the reception room, and a few minutes later the Imperial couple appeared, accompanied by their children, the Grand Duke Alexandrovich and the Grand Duchess Elisaveta Fyodorovna. Neither the Princess Kochubi nor the Court ladies, nor even the adjutants had been invited to this family luncheon. I alone had been thus distinguished!

This definitely proved to me that the Empress had ignored the gossip and that she continued to give me her confidence. After lunch, when I left the Palace to return to St. Petersburg, I was a happy and grateful creature.

That year the summer season at Peterhof was especially brilliant, chiefly because the Archduke Karl Ludwig of Austria and his sympathetic wife, Maria Theresia, had come for a protracted visit. Many parties were given in honor of the Archduchess, who was a great favorite in Russian society. Each party surpassed the next in taste and beauty. I remember as being particularly impressive, a ball in the White Room of the Palace; the night was very warm; all the windows were open and one could see the park with its fountains, and the dark ocean beyond.

Another party, conspicuous for its originality, was given by the Grand Duchess Eugenia Maximilianovna. The hall had been decorated to resemble a peasant's cottage. In an adjoining room were placed real cows, to complete the picture, and all the servants wore peasants' costumes. The whole arrangement was charming.

Late that Fall, I met the Archbishop Antonin, who had just been made Chancellor of the Seminary. I made his acquaintance at a religious gathering, and asked him how one should proceed in order to awaken a religious feeling among prisoners. Antonin showed himself interested in my problem at once, and gave me valuable advice.

I had already introduced the reading of religious literature in the prisons on my own initiative, and was pleased to see that this measure began to show some good results. We were, however, not able to explain the dogma to the prisoners, and so it was natural that I asked for the support of the clergy. In the course of our conversation the Archbishop and I also touched on problems of a more general nature, such as the interdependence of Church and State as founded by Peter the Great, and each time I was struck by the modesty and profound faith of this great dignitary. He was also deeply interested in the problem of Russian Sectarianism, and could not understand how these false doctrines could attract so many adherents. He came to the conclusion that the methods of instruction of the Orthodox Church must be faulty in some way, as they were unsatisfactory to so many people. "It will become necessary," he continued, "to reform religious education fundamentally." He was also opposed to any violent suppression of the sects, because, he explained, the Church should use only spiritual weapons.

The Emperor Alexander III also took note of these errors of faith, which persisted even despite the most severe punishments. In a conversation with the Metropolitan Platon, he once asked him what the cause of Sectarianism was.

"The people seek God, Your Majesty," answered the wise prelate, "and that manifestation is in itself a reproach to Orthodoxy. Our people thirst for spiritual light, and it is our duty to give it to them. Sheep don't run astray under the guidance of a good shepherd—but how many good shepherds are there in our Church?"

The Princess Volkonski and I had resumed our interest in the subject of the union between the Eastern and Western Church at that time. It had also been the pet theme of Vladimir Solovyev, whom I repudiated since he had made the audacious remark in his book, "Russia and the Universal Church," that he was speaking in the names of twenty million Russians. This phrase had led Rome to believe, for a time at least, that Russia could easily be won to Catholicism, with the aid of Solovyev and the Princess Volkonski. There also existed a fond hope that the Imperial ear might be reached through the mediation of the Princess Kochubi, who was Princess Volkonski's aunt. At the time, all these conjectures aroused my deep indignation, although my opinions in the matter of the Church problems have undergone a change since then and I am now beginning to believe that Solovyev's ideas were not entirely wrong.

CHAPTER XII

The Love Story of a Grand Duke—A Dramatic Scene with the Empress—The Helpful Crown Prince—A Railroad Accident in the Tsar's Family—The Empress Relates Her Horrible Experiences—I Go to Florence—Villa Ombrellino—"Boiars Russes en Voyage"—News About Michael Michailovich's Romance—The Last Intrigue of "Mentir Pasha."

ONE EVENING in February of 1887, the Grand Duke Michael Alexandrovich expressed the desire to spend an evening at my house together with his wife. I invited a few other gentlemen for that night, so that the Grand Duke might not miss his customary game of cards, and had made all arrangements for a pleasant evening for my august guests. But the Grand Duchess seemed worried and irritable when she arrived, and it did not take long before she explained why.

"Just think of it," she said, her voice trembling with annoyance, "Misha has taken it into his head to marry young Katya Ignatiev. He announced it to us formally. He, who falls in love with a new girl every week! Only recently he cried bitterly because his hopes of marrying the Princess Valeski had been frustrated, and now it's the little Ignatiev girl! We have the pleasure of witnessing his love dramas each time."

Just a few days after this, "Misha," the young Grand Duke, Michael Michailovitch, called on me and with characteristic frankness told me all about his romance. He was head over heels in love with the pretty, lively and somewhat flirtatious Katya Ignatiev, daughter of the former Secretary of State, and met her regularly in the homes of the Countesses Kiesenhausen and Ignatiev. He was under the impression that her father was not displeased with their relations and had made an offer of marriage to Katya spontaneously, without consulting his parents.

Katya had, of course, accepted at once, and the young Grand Duke had rushed to his father full of happy excitement and asked for his blessing. Michael Alexandrovich had said neither yes nor no, but had only remarked that he would have to talk it over with his wife. This sufficed to send the impetuous young man dashing over to the Empress in the Anichkov Palace, to fall on his knees before her there and beg for her consent. Confused and bewildered by the pathetic spectacle, the Empress had seized an icon and blessed the Grand Duke, whereupon the young man had disappeared muttering some disconnected words of thanks.

But on the following morning the storm broke. The Grand Duchess declared emphatically that she would not hear of the whole affair, that she did not believe in the permanence of this love, and that she saw in the entire matter nothing more than a temporary aberration of her son's. Not satisfied with this decisive declaration, she immediately drove to the Empress and explained matters to her as she saw them.

"Are there no more class distinctions in Russia?" she cried. "Today it is the pretty little Ignatiev girl; tomorrow it may be the daughter of a business man, and the day after that it may be a fairly well-educated servant girl. In this manner the Imperial Family must lose all its prestige."

Naturally this affair became the favorite theme of St. Petersburg society; further development of events was tensely awaited, and as usual, opinions were divided.

In the meantime the Grand Duke and his wife had decided to give their son a year of grace which he was to spend abroad. If, at the close of this year, his sentiments had remained unchanged, they would discuss the matter further. "You'll see," said the Grand Duchess to me at the time, "that in a year, his head will be full of other things."

From the very beginning the Grand Duke had treated the affair in a different manner from that in which his wife regarded it, so that she did not hesitate to suggest that he was acting under the spell of the young Countess Ignatiev. He answered that, in his opinion, Michael Michailovich ought to marry, and as he had not been successful with the Princess, it was not fair to forbid his marriage with Katya Ignatiev. The good Grand Duke was already picturing the way he would receive the young couple after their year of grace, and bless them. But he had forgotten to reckon with the energy of the Grand Duchess and the difficulties of Court life.

In the beginning of 1888 the young Grand Duke returned from abroad, but as the prescribed time had not yet elapsed he evaded all meetings with Katya, by way of fulfilling his promise. If both of them happened to be at some Court ball, the Grand Duke never entered the room in which his fiancée might be dancing, but played cards incessantly. In the circle of the young Grand Duke, everyone took his side, and it often happened that all the young men who took his part would toast his fiancée at their gay supper parties.

Michael Michailovitch often came to me to ease his heart in those days. "What shall I do to convince my parents of the permanence of my love?" he asked me regularly. I could only advise him to wait patiently until the allotted time had elapsed.

But months had gone by and the affairs of the young man showed no progress. The Grand Duchess declared that she would leave the decision to the Emperor, and so

Michael Michailovich went to him. He threw himself at the Emperor's feet and begged for his consent to the marriage. The Tsar told him to try for an understanding with "the ladies," which meant the Grand Duchess and the Empress. "If they agree to your marriage, I shall not deny you my consent."

In his trouble, the young Grand Duke even turned to the Crown Prince for aid. The latter not only encouraged him but also put in a good word for him to his father, the Emperor. Directly after his conversation with the Tsar, the Crown Prince sent the Grand Duke a note, telling him that prospects looked well. Michael Michailovich became enthusiastic, and with his customary exuberance told everyone that the Emperor had given his consent to the marriage and that no more obstacles lay in the way.

In reality, matters were not so favorable. The Grand Duchess insisted that she would not even discuss the affair, and that she had left all decisions to the Emperor. The Emperor in turn replied that he could not give his consent unless the parents had agreed upon the marriage, and so no definite result could be reached in this vicious circle.

In addition, the Emperor was very much preoccupied with the Bulgarian situation just then, and in no mood to solve the love problems of a young Grand Duke. Finally a family council was decided upon, and its word was to be final.

How often in those days was I called upon to dry the tears of Michael Michailovich—in the literal sense of the word! When he called on me and discussed his troubles with me, I could not help but give him all my sympathy, especially when he said to me. "My friends are advising me to drink and go to parties. But I detest all those things from the bottom of my heart. I don't wish to forget! I don't want to divert myself!"

I was not able to watch the progress of this romance during the Fall and following Winter, as I had become seriously ill again and had decided, upon the advice of my friends, to go abroad. While debating with myself where to go, I received a gracious invitation from my friend, N. N. Subov, to spend some time at her country place near Florence. Under the circumstances, the invitation was more than welcome.

I decided to go to Italy with my daughter in the beginning of 1890. In the meantime I left my son in the care of Prince Alexander Petrovich who solemnly promised to watch over him as over his own brother. Then, despite the general protestations, I resigned my office as President of the Prison Committee.

The preliminary preparations for the trip had taken up all of September, and it was on October 17th that the Princess of Oldenburg told me she had just received a telegram reporting the terrible accident—the derailment of the Imperial train, which was carrying the Tsar's whole family from the Crimea to St. Petersburg.

It was only later that we learned the whole extent of the catastrophe which the monarch and his family had escaped as if by a miracle. The cause of the disaster was, as had often before been the case, the Russian carelessness and lack of punctuality. At the Emperor's order, an immediate and careful investigation was started, which proved conclusively that there was no malicious intent at the bottom of the accident, for which reason the Emperor pardoned all parties concerned with the exception of the Minister of Transportation, who was dismissed from his office.

Shortly before my departure for Florence, I was received in Gachina, and again invited to lunch with the Imperial family. The Empress was still noticeably nervous, and related—with the evidence of an inner excitement—the terrible minutes she had passed after the derailment of the Imperial train. She had been thrown down the incline of the railroad dam and had seen the wreckage of the train hanging over her head threatening to drop down and crush her any minute. Released from this frightful situation, she had watched the work of the rescue party and told with pardonable pride about the unselfish help her sons had given them.

The little Grand Duchess Olga Alexandrovna had escaped death in the most miraculous manner. The impact at the moment of the derailment had flung her out of her nurse's arms through the window. In falling, she had cried in her delicate child's voice: "Dear God, don't let me die." She rolled down the slope and landed at the feet of the sentry. It developed that she was entirely unharmed, while the nurse was found crushed to death in the wreckage of the train.

Not a word about the accident was to be mentioned in the presence of the Tsar. He was so shaken up by the danger they had escaped, and by the deaths of so many loyal servants, that he did not want to hear another reference to the awful disaster.

My visit to Gachina took place at the beginning of the new year. I then handed the management of the Prison Committee over to my successor, the Countess Kuropatkin, and left for my trip abroad, ready for new impressions.

Villa Ombrellino, the Subov's country place, was situated on a prominence near Florence. The house had been built in the style of the most brilliant Italian artistic period. The Subov family had bought the Villa in 1874, and had equipped it with every modern convenience, including a Russian heating system, which kept the rooms and halls pleasantly warm even in the winter. At this beautiful place my friend surrounded me with the tenderest care, by keeping all work and worry away from me and so leaving me to devote myself to my health and to my daughter.

From my balcony I could see the valley of the Arno and the numerous villages, characteristically dotted with towers. A Franciscan monastery was situated near the villa and almost daily a monk in a brown cowl would come from there to perform services in the private chapel of Maria Nikolayevna. All this was so typically Italian that I fancied I was drinking in the atmosphere of this fairy country with the air I breathed. It was very rarely that I left our hill to go down to the city. There one encountered, as in all other cities of the world, only gossip, card-playing, smoking and the inevitable political discussions, which I had just left behind me.

The spring was unusually beautiful, even for Italy, and I spent the days visiting churches and museums with my daughter, and making excursions to Fiesole, Prato, and Pistoia. My daughter made an efficient guide. She had made it her business to study her books and maps thoroughly before we started, and we had no trouble in finding our way afterwards.

By the end of May, we left Florence, and went to Lake Como and to Bellagio, where we met the G——— family, old friends of ours. They represented the vanishing type of the "Boiars Russes en voyage," their party consisting of father, mother, four little children, a governess, a tutor, Russian maids, Russian butler, their Russian samovar and immense quantities of luggage. They were agreeable, cultured people, with whom we made enjoyable excursions and took pleasant walks.

We went by way of Lugano and Bozano to Baden-Baden, where we had planned to meet the Grand Duchess Olga Fyodorovna. I was very happy to see the Grand

Duchess, who had shown me so much sympathy, once more. Besides, my friend Alexandra Sergeyevna Oserov was in her train. I was less charmed, however, by the presence of the Chamberlain Emanuel Sergeyevitch Muchanov, who had never been sympathetic to me. He was very intelligent and cultured, a convinced atheist, cold-blooded and conceited. His beautiful, eternally immobile features reminded me of Mephisto. The Grand Duchess patronized this strange man of ironic speech, because she found him interesting, but the rest of the family were not especially attracted to him.

At Baden-Baden I stopped at the same Hotel Angleterre where I had stayed sixteen years before, directly before my daughter Vera was born. The Grand Duchess and her train stopped at the Hotel Stephanie.

Now I heard further news concerning young Michael Michailovich and his love affair. The Grand Duchess herself did not mention a word of it, but my friend Oserov had volumes to tell me. According to her report, the family council in the Imperial Palace, which had been awaited so anxiously, had decided against the marriage of the Grand Duke, thus shattering all his fond hopes.

She told me that the unhappy young man and his brother Georgiy Michailovich were at that moment in Heidelberg, and as I had intended to go to that city anyhow, in order to consult Professor Kussmaul, who was considered one of the greatest physicians in Germany, I set out for that city at once.

It was a beautiful spring morning when my daughter and I arrived in that interesting university town. We stopped at the same hotel in which the two Grand Dukes had their apartments, and I notified Count Grebbe, a friend of theirs, of my arrival immediately, and in this manner let the two young men know that I should like to see them as soon as possible.

When Georgiy Michailovich called on me, he at once plunged into the theme which was engrossing him passionately at the moment. This was the toast which the Tsar had proposed to the Prince of Montenegro, in which he called him "Russia's only friend." The Grand Duke was elated by this political demonstration, just as he was delighted by the marriage between Peter Nicolayevich and the Princess Militsa of Montenegro. "The only friend," he cried again and again. "How this must have annoyed all the others." . . . Neither Georgiy Michailovich nor I understood the real meaning of the Emperor's words at that time.

We all had tea together in a summer house in the garden and then Michael Michailovitch took me aside to open his heart to me. He was very much depressed as he told me how the family council had been deferred again and again, and how an unexpected event had suddenly given the whole affair a very distressing political turn.

It seems that one day a Bulgarian deputation had arrived in St. Petersburg to offer the Bulgarian throne—vacant at the time—to Michael Michaelovich! St. Petersburg realized at once that this offer was not being made to the unknown Grand Duke as such, but to the future son-in-law of the Count Ignatiev. Evidently certain circles in Sophia were figuring on the likelihood of seeing Count Ignatiev, the creator of Bulgaria, rule the country from behind the throne of his son-in-law. Or did there lurk behind all this a new move of old "Mentir Pasha" himself? The crafty diplomat was perfectly capable of playing a clever double game wherein he could convince the Bulgarians that the Tsar desired his future son-in-law to be crowned King of Bulgaria, and on the

Princess Yuryevskaya in the year 1875

Princess Dolgorukov-Yuryevskaya the morganatic wife of Alexander II

other hand, convince the Tsar that such was the desire of the Bulgarian people.

When the deputation arrived, Michael Michailovich had the tact not to receive it. But the family council, which finally met with the Emperor at its head, had grown still more skeptical in view of these new events and rumors.

The old Grand Duke Michael Alexandrovich was still optimistic enough to assume that under certain conditions his son might be permitted to make a morganatic marriage. In a conversation, he asked Michael Michailovitch which of these conditions he would be ready to accept, naming some of them: the renunciation of his title; banishment from Russia; changing his name, etc. But Michael answered: "Anything; I accept any condition—only I want Katya."

In the family council, the Grand Duke Vladimir Alexandrovich declared himself in favor of a morganatic marriage for Michael Michailovich, and his wife seconded him. The Tsarina and the Grand Duke Sergey Alexandrovich, however, were against it. When the Tsar then explained the whole extent of the Bulgarian intrigue to his family, they voted unanimously against the marriage. A union between any Imperial Prince and a Countess Ignatiev was politically too hazardous to permit of any consideration for the personal happiness of the young man. Thus State reasons had carried off the victory, and the plea of Michael Michailovitch was refused. The decision of the family council was put on record by Count Voronzov, the Court Secretary, and a copy of it was sent to every Grand Duke and to the Count Ignatiev.

Poor Michael Michailovich told me all this in the summer house of the hotel garden in Heidelberg. As we were alone, he didn't have to restrain his emotions, and so he sobbed out the description of the desperate mood into which the family decision had thrown him. His dejection had been so deep that his father had become anxious for his welfare and had made him promise not to commit any foolish act. . . . Michael Michailovich replied that he was too religious to do himself a bodily harm; but that his life was forever ruined by the cruel verdict of his family.

I was sincerely sorry for the desperate young man and consoled him as well as I could. I could not then foresee what a surprising turn this strange romance would take two years later, and what a tragedy was to develop from it.

CHAPTER XIII

An Interesting Marriage Scheme—Romanov and Orleans—Poor Tsar Nicholas—Field Marshal Archduke Albrecht—War Rumors in Vienna — Changed Conditions in Russia — A Venetian Festival in St. Petersburg—The Romance of the Grand Duke Takes an Astonishing Turn—The Tsar's Displeasure—The Death of the Grand Duchess Olga Fyodorvna —I Become a Court Lady of the Empress.

IN MARIENBAD where I was staying to continue my cure, after having left Heidelberg, I met many of my acquaintances, among others, Olga Alexeyevna Novikov, who had attracted considerable attention by her political articles which were written in English. She belonged to the Slavophile Party, and during her frequent visits to England was trying to dissipate the foreign prejudice against Russia by her pamphlets and articles, in which she pictured her country as it really was. Our Minister of State was very much pleased with her activities, as it seemed a most desirable thing at that time, to influence English public opinion to a favorable view of Russia.

It was through Olga Novikov that I also met General Gallifet, who had come to Marienbad accompanied by the "Countess of Paris." Gallifet had imperiled his reputation by his severity in 1871, when he had ordered seventeen hundred revolutionists to be executed.

He told me that his wife desired to make my acquaintance, which surprised me. Although I had met him many years before at the home of the Countess de Valence, I could not assume that he had remembered me after such a long interval of time sufficiently to tell his wife about me. It didn't take me long to discover that the Countess was more interested in my position at the Russian Court than in myself as a person. At that time, the Grand Duke Nicolai Michailovich was in Paris, considering marriage with the charming Princess Helene of Orleans. Negotiations had already been started with the Vatican, and the Pope had intimated that he would be willing to give his consent to this union of a Catholic Princess and a member of the Orthodox Imperial Family.

Later in the year, after I had returned to St. Petersburg, the Grand Duchess Olga Fyodorovna showed me a letter from her son which she had just received. In it he asked his mother for directions as to his future attitude; he had been invited to their Castle Eu by the Orleans family, and was perfectly aware that acceptance or refusal of this invitation would mean either a formal proposal of marriage to the Princess, or the tacit withdrawal of his suit. He did not want to make such an important decision without having consulted his mother.

After mature consideration, the Grand Duchess told me that she knew very well that her son would never marry the French Princess if he had been forbidden to do so, and in fact might never marry at all, for he disliked the German Princesses who were the only other choices to be considered as far as marriage was concerned. He was always making fun of them.

"What has the Grand Duke to say?" I asked.

"He says his father, the Tsar Nicholas I, would turn in his grave if he knew that his grandson was thinking of marrying the granddaughter of the Citizen King. The old Tsar would never have regarded such a marriage as valid." And smiling, she added that the good old Tsar had probably had to turn over a good many times already and that one more turn would not matter. "But," she said, "I am afraid of the smooth intrigues and the propaganda of the Catholic Party."

The carriage of Alexander II, wrecked by the bomb of the assassin

The Study of Alexander III in the Kremlin

The Spot on which Alexander II was assassinated

Finally, the entire affair was put into the Emperor's hands, who decided that Nicolai Michailovich was not to accept the invitation to Castle Eu. In this manner, the whole project which, if it had been carried out, would undoubtedly have had important consequences, was dismissed.

During my stay in Marienbad I also made the acquaintance of the old Austrian Field Marshal, Archduke Albrecht, the victor of Custoza. He liked to flirt with the young girls, and between times would join the party at our table and have his dinner with us.

A Viennese lady who often joined our group, once said to me, pointing to the Grand Duke, "That is our military commandant, who will lead our armies against yours in case of war."

Quite amazed, I asked her if a war was imminent, whereupon she answered that a war between Austria and Russia was inevitable, and that she only hoped it might be deferred as long as possible. Certainly the words of a lady who was not too well informed on political matters were not to be taken seriously, and yet I realized that the possibility of a war with Russia was being discussed in Austrian Government circles. It was only now that I began to see what danger it would have signified to Russia had Count Ignatiev's bold combination succeeded, and I realized the wisdom of our Emperor who had avoided these political complications by his decision. Compared with the immeasurable disaster of a war, the personal fate of the young Grand Duke Michael Michailovich had to be regarded as negligible.

After my cure had been successfully finished, we returned to Russia, stopping in St. Petersburg for a short while only, and then visited my sister in the Major's Court. For the two last months of Autumn, we hired a villa in Tsarskoye Selo. The castle of Pavlovsk was occupied by the Grand Duchess Alexandra Yosefovna just then, together with her family and the Grand Duke who was quite ill. The latter had suffered a stroke of apoplexy during the previous Winter, just as the marriage ceremony between his granddaughter, the Greek Princess Alexandra Georgyevna, and the Grand Duke Paul Alexandrovich was being concluded. A subsequent stroke had robbed him of the powers of speech and locomotion, so that he had to be wheeled around in a little cart. He, who had formerly been such a brilliant and entertaining conversationalist, was now mute although perfectly conscious, and was only able to emit brute sounds, the meaning of which no one could understand.

As would be expected under such circumstances, the castle bore a gloomy and unhappy air; the Grand Duchess Alexandra Yosefovna avoided appearing before her husband, because her presence made him very nervous. She sought consolation in the loving attentions of her children who did everything to assuage their mother's grief in her time of trial.

The unhappy patient lay in a side wing of the castle and slept beneath the watchful eye of his adjutant, or gave vent to those dreadful sounds, which no one understood nor wished to understand.

When I returned to St. Petersburg for the winter season, I noticed that some changes had taken place at Court. The Princess Kochubi had died in February of 1888, and had been replaced by the Countess Anna Dimitryevna Stroganov. Besides this, a new smaller court had formed through the marriage of the Grand Duke Paul Alexandrovich. When I paid my respects to the young Grand Duchess Alexandra Georgyevna, she seemed to me a very charming lady, apparently yearning for her sunny Greece on that gloomy November day;

she looked very pale and suffered considerably during her pregnancy.

"Mish-Mish," as we called Michael Michailovich, was still abroad. The family had extracted a promise from him to undertake nothing whereby he might be forced into a marriage with Katya Ignatiev. The temporary calm of his stormy romance withdrew it from the limelight in Court circles for a while.

The Winter passed with its usual procession of receptions and divers festivities, of which the Venetian Fiesta given by the Grand Duchess Katharina stands out prominently in my memory. The Princess Helen had taken over the musical management and conducted the chorus—composed of amateurs—with great vivacity. The most attractive part of this party was the banquet, faithfully copied after Titian's famous painting. The most beautiful women of the Capital were invited to take part in this *tableau vivant,* the most eminent artists and connoisseurs had studied and coached the performance to its smallest detail, with a central committee composed of Rubinstein, Lingard and Count Sologub. The plan was very intricate, as a performance of historic dances was to follow the banquet. This meant countless rehearsals, and almost every night a large company was gathered in the Michael Palace for this purpose. We were all very happy, when we began to notice how an artistic ensemble was gradually developing from the original chaos. In view of all the work and trouble involved, the performance proper was a perfect success.

One Sunday in March when I came to the Palais Michael for luncheon as usual, I found the Grand Duchess in an unusually sparkling mood. She told me laughingly that some people had tried to persuade her to go to a Gypsy restaurant some night and listen to their famous music. Then we spoke of her planned trip to the Crimea, and the Grand Duchess suggested that I spend a few weeks of rest again in her unoccupied Castle Pavlovsk. When I parted from her that day so cheerfully I little imagined what a shock was in store for her.

On the following day, the Grand Duke Nicolai Michailovich received Count Grebbe, who had just arrived from Cannes, and who was the bearer of several letters from Michael Michailovich to the members of the Imperial family. In these letters, the young Grand Duke informed them that several weeks previously he had married the Countess Meerenberg. The secret had been so well guarded, that up to that time no one knew anything about it, with the exception of the mother of the clever young lady. Michael Michailovich begged his brother to inform their parents of his independent step as gently as possible.

When the Grand Duchess returned from her drive that day, the Grand Duke Nicolai Michaelovich rushed downstairs to meet her with his brother's letter. One can imagine how the news crushed her spirit!

When I arrived at the Anichkov Palace the following morning to view the parade of the Equestrian Guard, I knew nothing of these events. But when I saw the Grand Duchess after the parade was over, I noticed at once the unusual redness of her generally pale countenance, and the ominous lustre in her eye. As soon as she noticed me, she came up to me and said: "I suppose you don't know yet what a surprise Misha has given us—he is married!"

"Married?" I cried, utterly taken aback. "The little Ignatiev?"

"Not at all. The little Meerenberg girl! Evidently she is his new passion. I told you from the very beginning that he never knows what he wants. The worst of it, however, is that he promised the Emperor to do nothing of this sort—and now, he has broken his promise!"

It was the last mentioned circumstance that aroused the greatest indignation of his parents; they feared the Tsar's displeasure. And indeed, this fear proved quite justified. The Emperor deprived the young man of the right to wear his adjutant's tunic, and took the captaincy of his regiment away from him. These penalties were meted out to the Grand Duke in one day, and His Majesty's orders concerning them were published in the daily press.

The Grand Duke Michael Alexandrovich, a soldier to the core, suffered deeply under this disciplining of his son. When I dined with the ducal couple a few days later, prior to their departure, the Grand Duke maintained an unbroken silence throughout the entire meal, while his wife spoke incessantly of their son in tones of sarcastic scorn.

"You can imagine," the Grand Duke said to me later, "how this affects me. I suffer frightfully!"

I looked at him pityingly, and asked him why he tolerated this subject of conversation which annoyed him so much. "Because," he answered, "it is a relief for my wife to be able to speak about it. For me it is deadly."

I stayed alone with the Duchess until about ten o'clock that night, and she opened her heart further to me. Then she said good-bye very graciously, almost affectionately, and left town that same night.

Her train had hardly gotten as far as Kharkov when she suffered a heart attack and was forced to discontinue her journey. Her condition grew steadily and rapidly worse, so that her husband was called to her bedside by telegraph. But when the Grand Duke and her sons arrived in Kharkov it was too late. She died on March 31st, without having seen any one of her family before she passed away. Her death was a tragic sequel to the romance of Michael Michailovich.

Michael Michailovich's relations with his family grew still more strained, when, under the influence of his mother-in-law, he refused to attend the funeral of the Grand Duchess. The old Countess Meerenberg doubted the young husband's strength of character, and feared that under the persuasion of his family, he might be moved to declare his marriage void. . . . Anyone acquainted with Michael Michailovich would have had to admit that she was right from her standpoint, but this affront brought about a complete rupture with the Imperial Family.

When I heard the sad news, I traveled from Moscow to Kharkov immediately, and there met the newly made widower at his wife's bier. We all attended the funeral masses which were read twice a day, and I noted with satisfaction that the Grand Duke's deep religious feeling helped him through the hardest days of mourning. Then he resolutely turned to the discharge of his official duties once more. I, too, felt deeply the loss of this woman whose kindly sympathy had supported me in my darkest hours.

Shortly after the funeral I suddenly and quite unexpectedly received a picture of the Empress, and my appointment as Court lady. As I was entitled to this privilege neither by age nor by position, the distinction conferred upon me by Her Majesty in this way filled me with pleasure and satisfaction. My enemies were thrown into approximately the same degree of excitement by this appointment, incidentally. I wrote to the Empress at once, of course, to thank her for the great honor conferred on me.

CHAPTER XIV

An Attack on the Crown Prince—The Home of a Real Russian Noble—Famine In the Country—Aid From Count Tolstoy—Debates on Catholicism vs. Orthodoxy—Father Augustin's Carriere—A Visit From Johann of Kronstadt—A Pilgrimage of the Pious Peasants—An Embarrassing Argument—The Building of a Village Church.

On April 29th, which was the birthday of the Grand Duke Sergei Alexandrovich, we all gathered in his palace. This day also signified the end of the Grand Duke's stay among us, for he had been called to fill the post of Governor-General in Moscow, and from now on his palace would remain empty. His chief stewardess, too, was at her post for the last time that day. She had accepted Catholicism and as a Catholic she could not continue to serve the Grand Duke in the orthodox city of Moscow.

During the holidays, Her Majesty invited me to Gachina, and as always I was happy to go. What was my consternation upon my arrival, to find the Empress in tears! I soon learned their cause when she showed me a telegram to the effect that the Tsar, who at that moment was in Japan together with the Crown Prince, had been attacked by an assassin, and that in the encounter, the Crown Prince had received a sabre-cut across his head. The vagueness of the telegram threw the Empress into greatest unrest. She was afraid her son's wound might be more serious than the telegram indicated. Fortunately it developed that her fears were groundless, and the dangerous event had no further consequences. However the scar on the Crown Prince's head remained always visible, almost as if to remind the future Emperor constantly of the treachery of the Japanese people.

In the beginning of the Summer I went to Moscow with my son in order that he might make the most of his vacation. We visited a French exhibit which was being held in Moscow that year, and ate in those restaurants where the famous gypsy bands played, and inspected all the historic sights and landmarks of the old Coronation city.

Then Kira left to join his regiment, while my daughter Vera and I visited our friends the Baryatinskis at their estate Grunovka, on the borders of the Kursk and Kharkov Governments. This place was remarkable not only for its location but also for its elegant living quarters and stables, and was rightfully considered one of the most beautiful country estates in all Russia. The large mansion, built on a terrace, had a fine art gallery, which contained works of famous masters, family portraits, and statues, as well as a voluminous and well-catalogued library. Small gardens grew about the house, merging directly into the immense oak forest. Prince Baryatinski had beautiful roads laid through it, so that one could drive for hours in the magnificent woods.

Our stay in Grunovka was a time of unceasing delight to me. It was not only that nature was so rich in beauty here, but the artistic and intellectual atmosphere which permeated this home spun a web of enchantment around me. The Prince would often read to us from the correspondence between his brother and the Emperor Alexander II, in which political problems were aptly discussed. Couched in model French, these letters from the Field Marshal contained respectful but frank criticism of the Tsar's decisions at times, while the letters from Alexander II showed the latter's anxious desire for the welfare of the nation in every detail.

The Coronation of Alexander III in Moscow

Tsar Alexander III, as Crown Prince and his wife Maria Fyodorovna

Thus the Summer passed very pleasantly, and with the approach of Autumn I began preparations to introduce my daughter to society. She made friends quickly among the young people, who liked her for her childlike nature and her earnest modesty, and last but not least for her understanding of scientific problems. Her pretty face with its great black eyes was very attractive.

The social season suffered some restraint that Fall and Winter, however. The great famine of that year, which was spreading over several governments made it advisable to countermand the official festivities. The reports from the provinces regarding the economic condition of the peasants were growing desperate. The Government assisted them as well as it could, and private groups organized relief funds. Their center was a relief station founded by Count Leo Nicolayevich Tolstoy.

After leaving my daughter with friends at Tsarskoye Selo, I went to Her Majesty at Peterhof for a day and then for two days to Oranienbaum to visit the Grand Duchess Katharina. After that I hurried to our Stepanovski estate where my friend the Princess Elisaveta Georgyevna Volkonski was to be my guest. She had had to leave her own estate Pavlovskoye, because the cholera had broken out in its vicinity, and I was delighted to be her hostess for a few weeks.

She had brought with her the manuscript of her book on the Church in which she refuted the objections of the Ecclesiastical Academy to her first book. She read some passages to me and I was compelled to admire not only her scintillating mind but also her wealth of information on religious matters and historical data. I believe that at that time her conversion to Catholicism was not complete, but I quickly realized that even then she belonged body and soul to the Roman Church. Her conversation showed plainly that she had never fully penetrated into the true structure and inner content of Orthodoxy, and it occurred to me that it might be interesting to arrange a discussion between her and Father Augustin.

This Father Augustin, a former Benedictine monk, was in every respect a notable personality. He was a descendant of a family of French counts, and had strayed to Kiev by accident. It was here that he had become acquainted with the doctrines and rituals of the Orthodox Church. Difficult as it had been for him to separate from his parents and country, he nevertheless had followed the call of his convictions, and entered an Orthodox convent. Transplanted into a foreign land, whose very language he barely controlled, and the climate and living conditions of which were new and strange to him, he earnestly and patiently sought to lead an existence consonant with his new convictions. He succeeded, and his kindness attracted many friends to him in Kiev.

Eighteen years later, the Chief Procurator of the Synod, the all powerful Pobyedonostzev, came to Kiev at the occasion of a celebration anent the ninth centenary of the Russian Christian Church. His attention was directed to modest Father Augustin, and Pobyedonostzev, always eager to encourage talented and efficient priests, promoted him to a higher ecclesiastical post in St. Petersburg at once where, shortly after, I made his acquaintance.

There he occupied three rooms in the building of the Synod, which were stacked with books from floor to ceiling. The rarest and costliest editions were numbered among these, usually bought at the sacrifice of the major portion of his none too generous salary. We became friends at once, and he even spent a whole Summer at Stepanovski as my guest.

My plan to induce him into a refutation of the Princess Volkonski's views did not materialize, however. Father

Augustin was feeling ill and tired, and besides he was working on a scientific study of the early Christian era. The collecting and assembling of the necessary material so absorbed his time and attention, that he had to refuse my proposal, politely but firmly.

On the same day that Lisa Volkonski left me after our supper and after a fervent prayer in my small private chapel, I received a telegram announcing the imminent visit of Father Johann of Kronstadt, in answer to an invitation I had sent the reverend priest. His coming was deeply gratifying to me as I had not quite dared believe that he would actually honor me with his visit.

I knew that my guest would need to rest on his arrival, and therefore did everything in my power to keep his visit a secret. My inspector had strict orders not to mention a word of it to anyone. Consequently no attention was attracted when Father Johann drove up before our house. I was standing on the balcony awaiting his arrival and hurried down to receive him. But I had hardly greeted him when he told me that he would have to leave on the following morning.

"Really!" I cried in my disappointment. "You have only just arrived and are already preparing to leave us. Where are you going?"

"Back to St. Petersburg. On my way back, I'd like to visit a certain convent, and then I have to go to Reval, via St. Petersburg. I am dedicating a cathedral there on August 15th. The Governor, Prince Shakhovskoy, has asked this of me especially," he answered.

"Little Father, I don't know how to thank you. At the same time, I am embarrassed to think that you have made this wearisome trip just to please me."

"That's nothing," he answered, full of loving-kindness, "I can rest during the drive, and besides it is a pleasure to me to visit you."

We were not able to chat for long; for though Father Johann had not been recognized immediately on his arrival, the report of his presence had soon become known. Everyone came running. The peasants left their work in the fields, carriages and all sorts of vehicles began to move, and crowds of pedestrians filled the roads leading to our house. Merchants, priests, monks, the ill, the lame—they all came from the most remote villages, so that the local police became excited.

I immediately offered our chapel for services, which was not only filled to the last seat in no time but the masses overflowed into the court where they all stood bareheaded, while Father Johann read from the Holy Writ.

Toward evening the crowd dispersed, and proceeded to camp on our grounds, for Father Johann had promised to read a morning service before his departure, and of course no one thought of going home that night. In the meantime a few friends and neighbors had gathered about the godly man in my salon, and he chatted animatedly with them all. Among these guests was the Igumen Arseniy from the Starzesk Convent, who tactlessly questioned our dear guest in a way which embarrassed me by its lack of good breeding. He asked Father Johann, who had been his teacher, by what means he had attained his present office, to which Father Johann answered briefly and calmly that he had never had a teacher outside the books of the great Church Fathers, and that the strength of his prayers had been his only guide.

But to my great despair, the Igumen would not be silenced.

"Do you know," he said, "that you are on a dangerous path? Your fame is spreading all over the world and is already greater than that of the Saviour. Only the small country of Palestine spoke about Him in His day,

Tsar Alexander III

Tsarina Maria Fyodorovna

but you are known all over the globe—even in America! Do you know the sentence: 'Woe to you if your name be greater than your deeds'?"

Far from growing angry at this rudeness, Father Johann answered with such restraint and modesty that the Igumen became calm and finally begged Father Johann to confess him.

Throughout the night we heard the jingling of bells as wagon after wagon arrived from the vicinity. Some of the people sought shelter among my servants, and those who did not find any slept in the open fields until the hour of daybreak. When the morning service was about to begin a mass of several thousand faithful souls crowded about the chapel, including in their number the ill, the deaf, the mute and the lame. Father Johann spoke to all who came to him, walked among the people and answered all their questions patiently. I finally succeeded in separating him from the crowd and brought him into my study for a few minutes. After carefully locking the door and drawing the curtains, I had to persuade him to sit down and implored him not to spend himself to exhaustion.

"I have to read a mass every day," he answered calmly, "and when I feel that the Holy Ghost is really about me in my prayer, I can go anywhere that day, into castles or into huts. But if that has not been the case, I receive no one, because without the grace of the Spirit, I do not feel the power to help others."

After Father Johann had left us, I summoned the peasants and disclosed a plan to them, which I had long been considering and which I had discussed with the holy man. I wanted to dissolve the affiliation of our parish with the neighboring community, which was entirely too large. Instead, I proposed a church for our own district, as we used to have in the old days. The peasants were very much interested in this idea and after the necessary formalities were over, everyone helped with the building of the church. Some loaned their horses for carting the building materials, some helped with the actual construction work, and others contributed money. So that two years later, when the church was dedicated, it actually represented the united efforts of the community.

CHAPTER XV

The Betrothal of the Grand Duchess Xenia Alexandrovna —Critical Illness of the Tsar—The Crown Prince's Marriage Plans—Original Reticence of the Tsarina—William II as Marriage Mediator—Advice From Queen Victoria—Farewell to the Dying Emperor—The Last Days of Alexander III.

THE FIRST social event of the year 1893 was the engagement of the Tsar's daughter, Xenia Alexandrovna, to the Grand Duke Alexander Michailovich. Not that this announcement came as a surprise, for the union had long been foreseen—yet it aroused a general feeling of joy, especially as the parents of both the young people had always desired their marriage.

Yet the Empress proved a typical mother by growing jealous at the thought of giving her child to a man. She conversed on this subject with me at great length, knowing that I had gone through the same experience only a short time before, when I married my daughter to Count Dimitri Nikolayevich Tatishchev, and that I was in sympathy with her state of mind.

But in the meantime a dark cloud was descending on the Court atmosphere. When the Emperor returned from Denmark in the Fall, he did not look well, and symptoms seemed to indicate a serious illness. He had grown thinner, his face was pale and his eyes reflected a great weariness. Recurrent attacks of nosebleeds seemed—in the opinion of the doctors—to point to the beginning of liver trouble.

In addition, that Winter the Emperor was stricken with influenza, and it became necessary to summon the famous doctor Sakharvin from Moscow. This grave fact was kept a secret from the public, but rumors seeped through to the effect that the physician considered the Emperor's condition critical and that it was primarily imperative for the Tsar to have complete rest. Assuming that a knowledge of the facts would insure the Emperor's compliance to this rule, Sakharvin did not spare him but informed him truthfully of the seriousness of his condition. Unfortunately the effect of this step was not what the physician had expected. At first, the Tsar became very depressed, and then decided to devote the short time left to him in this world to the discharge of the imminent, pressing obligations before him.

The Tsar's illness necessitated another quick decision in regard to an important and delicate matter. The successor to the throne, Nicolai Alexandrovich, intended to marry the Princess Alice of Hessia. So far there had been no final decision about their marriage, but the imminent danger of the Tsar's demise demanded prompt action.

Princess Alice had made her first visit to Russia at the age of twelve, for her sister Elizabeth's marriage to the Grand Duke Sergey Alexandrovich. Since then, she had visited her sister in Russia twice, once in St. Petersburg, and once at the latter's estate in Ilyinsk. It had even then been rumored that she was chosen as the future wife of the Crown Prince.

Her sister, the Grand Duchess Elizabeth, as well as the Court of Darmstadt, were pleased with the prospect, but the Empress remained in a negative state of mind, at first, because she feared to expose her son to foreign influences. She even forbade the Crown Prince to go to Ilyinsk at the time that he was supposed to meet Alice there.

The fact that the Crown Prince indeed did not come, in obedience to his mother's wishes, offended the ambitious Princess Alice deeply. She thought that her hopes of becoming the future Empress of Russia had been shattered thereby, and returned to Darmstadt profoundly disappointed. There she began to prepare for her confirmation.

But as it happened, the Crown Prince was unable to forget the Hessian Princess, and definitely refused all other proposals of marriage, so that the Empress found herself constrained to take steps toward negotiating for her son's betrothal.

One can imagine the astonishment of the St. Petersburg court, when Darmstadt replied with a polite refusal. The Princess Alice explained her non-acceptance by the fact that she had been confirmed already, and that consequently she could not now be converted to the Orthodox faith.

Far from accepting this explanation, the Crown Prince decided to take prompt action, and went to Hessia at once, where a number of august guests happened to be assembled. Besides several German Princes and Princesses, Queen Victoria of England and Wilhelm II were present. At first Alice firmly adhered to her original decision but Wilhelm II contrived to remain alone with the young couple and the Grand Duchess Maria Pavlovna in the salon. After a while the Grand Duchess and William II disappeared, and the tête à tête between the young people thus accomplished, brought about the desired results. Alice promised to reconsider the Crown Prince's offer, and to talk the matter over with her grandmother, Queen Victoria.

It was not difficult for the Queen to convince Alice that her conversion to the Orthodox Church could be effected without any qualms of conscience, for was there such a great difference between the two Christian creeds? Did not the Protestants as well as the Orthodox believe in the same Christ and the same Gospel?

By this time the Princess had given her consent, and had already begun to study the rudiments of the Byzantine faith under the tutorship of Father Basarov who was the official priest of the Russian Embassy at Stuttgart at that time. But when it became evident that Father Basarov was unable to cope with the influence which the Protestant pastors had exercised over the Princess, it was decided to send Father Yanyshev to her. He finally convinced the young girl definitively of the truth of the Orthodox faith. This had been—as he later told me—no easy task, for he was forced to discover time and time again the soundness of the Princess's religious education.

In the Spring of 1894, the engagement of the Crown Prince was officially announced, and a few months later the marriage of the Grand Duchess Xenia Alexandrovna to the Grand Duke Alexander Michailovich was celebrated in Peterhof. The Tsar was able to be present on that occasion, but his sickly appearance was a shock to everyone. This should not have been surprising, for all that Winter one ball had followed another until Easter time, and for some indefinable reason the Emperor, despite the doctor's orders, had not spared his attendance at any of these functions.

How often at these festivities, as I sat at the Emperor's table during supper would my eyes follow him sadly, as he walked from table to table greeting his friends amiably, and trying to hide the tired dull lustre of his eyes with a kindly smile. I knew that these parties tired him, especially as he would often work late into the night. Often drops of perspiration rose on his forehead, and he was repeatedly on the verge of fainting.

Yet he insisted upon examining the Cabinet's reports as always in the past, until the Empress called the members of the Ministry to her, and begged them to spare the Emperor and show him only the most urgent and important documents. "Report only the essential part of any business to him," she pleaded. "Don't forget that he is very ill and cannot stand the strain of too much work."

When the Empress told me of this conversation with the members of the Cabinet, she added with pensive sadness that only Delionov had shown any understanding or sympathy. "All the others were primarily interested in their personal influence, and consideration for the health and life of the Tsar was of secondary importance to them."

I saw Alexander III for the last time at a gala performance at the theatre in Peterhof. Tables had been placed in the park in front of the theatre, and tea was served there during the intermission. The Emperor surprised me by suddenly seating himself at my table. Our chat turned to the marriage of the Grand Duchess Xenia Alexandrovna.

"I know," he said, smiling, "how difficult it was for you to part with your daughter. You will naturally understand why the Empress and I feel a bit melancholy sometimes without our daughter."

When I begged His Majesty to permit me to leave on the same evening, as I wanted to return to my estate, he said, "Are you going to the country? How lucky you are! It must be lovely there at this time—and quiet—one might recover there."

His voice was filled with an unspeakable weariness—it gave me a pang! He, who had never believed in lassitude or tiredness, spoke thus! I told him that my daughter was expecting me in the country, whereupon he said that he knew how much I loved to see her. Then we parted, he with the most cordial words, and I with the premonition that I would never see him again.

His condition become so serious soon after this, that he left Tsarkoye Selo immediately after the grand parade, to rest in Livadia in the Crimea. But even there, his disease made such alarming progress that not only the most famous physicians but even Father Johann of Kronstadt himself were called to his bedside.

When Alice of Hessia arrived in Livadia, the Tsar made one more effort to receive his future daughter-in-law personally. A few days later, on October 20, 1894, he died. Rarely has the death of a monarch caused such widespread mourning as that of Alexander III.

CHAPTER XVI

Sad Entry of the Tsarina into the Capital—The Empress Alexandra Receives Me for the First Time—Preparations for the Coronation—Arrival At Moscow—I Am Entrusted With a Responsible Office—Dress Rehearsal of the Coronation—The Clumsy Hair-Dresser—Great Festivities In Moscow—Betrothal of the Italian Crown Prince—The Catastrophe on the Khodynski Field—Indignation of the Grand Dukes—The Imperial Couple Goes Abroad.

THE FORMER Princess Alice of Hessia, now Alexandra Fyodorovna, wife of the new Emperor of Russia, arrived at the Russian capital together with the funeral cortège, which brought the body of the late Tsar to St. Petersburg. Her marriage to Nicholas Alexandrovich took place in the Winter Palace on November 14, 1894. The young Empress, tall, slim and distinguished in appearance, looked so impressive that the Emperor seemed almost insignificant beside her. The Lady of State and First Lady-In-Waiting to the new Tsarina was the old Princess Galitzine, a very imposing lady, who had been brought up in the spirit of Nicholas I and who was opposed to all liberal ideas.

Directly after the marriage ceremony the young Imperial couple went to the Anichkov Palace and there took possession of the small apartments in which the Tsar and his brother George had lived during their childhood. A few days later the Empress began to receive her court ladies in rotation, and I had the honor to be the first to be presented to Her Majesty.

She made an agreeable impression on me at once, though I quickly noticed that her almost morbid shyness prevented her from acting as freely and naturally as she ordinarily would have. The consciousness of her exalted position seemed to fluster her, and her nervousness during these receptions caused her face to break out in red blotches which came and went, and made her nod her head convulsively as she spoke. It was difficult for her to find the proper words in conversation, or to speak in an easily flowing, pleasant manner.

Many interpreted this as arrogance, and accordingly a party which was hostile to her soon formed, the members of which inclined conspicuously to the Empress Mother, the wordly wise, ever charming Maria Fyodorovna.

The time for the formal Coronation in Moscow was approaching. But even during the preparations preceding it, difficulties and disagreements had begun to crop up. The Grand Duke Sergei Alexandrovich, who was Governor-General of Moscow and brother-in-law of the new Tsarina, had set his heart on making all the arrangements for the coronation. He was keenly disappointed in this ambition when he discovered that the Court Ministry had reserved the chief functions for its own. Deeply hurt, he declared that in that case he would leave all responsibility on the shoulders of the Ministry, though as Governor of Moscow, certain local arrangements were part of his office and, besides, he himself would leave the city. The Tsar was greatly embarrassed by this conflict, and tried to mediate between the two contestants. He succeeded in bringing about a compromise, whereby some of the arrangements fell to the Grand Duke and others to the Court Ministry. This actually unmotivated separation of activities contributed not a little to the general confusion, the consequence of which was the fatal catastrophe on the Khodynski Field.

In April, I too went to Moscow and there stopped at

the family residence of the Kurakins at the Red Gate, in the home of my brother. On the same day on which Their Majesties were to arrive in Moscow, the Princesses Vassilchikov and Baryatinski called on me suddenly. They brought the news that the Princess Galitzine had suffered a fall and hurt her foot, and was therefore unable to get to Moscow to perform her court duties. Their Majesties had asked me to act as her substitute in the capacity of First Lady-In-Waiting until she had fully recovered.

I was somewhat terrified at this summons, as I knew practically nothing about the details of the Coronation ceremony. But a refusal was impossible, and in my despair I decided to speak to the Empress and ask her to advise me.

On the following morning I drove to the Peter Palace where Their Majesties intended to stay until their ceremonial entry into the Kremlin. At first the guard would not let me enter, as I had no pass with me; but as soon as I gave my name, and explained that the Empress had summoned me, they made way for me. The Empress received me very graciously, gave me some directions, and placed the rooms which had been assigned to the Princess Galitzine at my disposal.

After this audience, I went to seek the Chamberlain Count Benckendorff, and told him of my new office. Then I drove to the Kremlin and paid my respects to the Countess Straganov, First Lady-In-Waiting to the Empress Mother, and talked with her about the necessity for our joint coöperation.

A few days later the State entry of Their Imperial Majesties into the Kremlin took place; the entire suite took part in it. The Tsar, as well as all foreign princes and all the Grand Dukes were on horseback, while the ladies together with the Empress Mother drove in gold carriages. It was a gorgeous picture, especially when the assembled populace began to shout and cheer Their Majesties as they passed the Red Gate.

The day of the Coronation was approaching, and the Princess Galitzine had not yet arrived in Moscow. My presentiment that the task of fastening the crown on the Empress's head would fall to me, filled me with growing anxiety. I remembered how at the Coronation of Alexander III, the Lady of State had fumbled in securing the crown on the head of the Tsarina, and I trembled.

My presentiment grew into a certainty, when the Empress summoned me and asked me to rehearse the moment of placing the crown on her head. "The Princess Galitzine is not coming," she said. "I am afraid you will have to do it. Come into my dressing room with me."

The Tsar was there when we entered. He was evidently very nervous, smoking one cigarette after another. The Empress's hair-dresser was there too. On the table stood a large etui, and presently the Emperor opened it and took from it the Imperial crown, covered with diamonds. He placed it on his wife's head, and the hairdresser stepped up to her, took up a diamond-studded hairpin and, explaining its manipulation to me, stuck it into the Empress's hair. She uttered a piercing scream, and jumped from the chair. . . . It developed that she had a very sensitive nerve on that very spot, and that the slightest touch caused her the most exquisite pain.

Terrified, I asked myself: "If even the hair-dresser who combs her hair every day can make this slip, what about me?"

The fastening of the Coronation robe proved still more difficult: on account of its rich gold and jewel ornaments it was extremely heavy and had to be fastened under the chin in the most intricate manner. Although Countess Geringer, the Lady of the Robes, explained the sequence of its manipulation to me in minute detail, and although I practiced and memorized these proceedings, I was by no means sure of myself.

Fortunately, everything went well, and without accident at the Coronation. Accompanied by the Princess Baryatinski, the Baroness Budberg, and the Countess Pahlen, who had been appointed Lady of State for this occasion, I mounted the dais. The Empress fell on her knees, the Tsar placed the crown on her head, and recalling the incident of the previous day, he whispered to me, "Careful!" I actually succeeded in avoiding the sensitive spot on her head, and also managed to fasten the Coronation robe in time, and stepped down from the platform relieved and grateful.

That evening when I had returned to my apartment, I looked out of the window and enjoyed an impressive picture: the tower of the Church of Ivan the Great was so brilliantly illuminated that it seemed as if steeped in a sea of fire, and its reflection made my room as bright as day.

The festivities following the Coronation took their scheduled course, but they terminated in an unexpected event of considerable political importance. The young Italian Crown Prince met the Princess Helen of Montenegro at this occasion, and fell in love with her. Upon his return from Moscow, he informed his parents that he intended to marry her. At first Their Italian Majesties objected to a union with the small princely house of Montenegro, which they did not consider their equal, but as the prince insisted on his choice the King gave his consent.

A great public festival at the Khodynski Field had been scheduled for May 18th, and gifts were to be distributed to the masses. One can imagine the shock at our arrival there, when we were told of a frightful catastrophe which had taken place in the forenoon.

Because of the inadequate organization, the pressing populace had swelled into a stampede and many thousands of people had been pushed into a deep ditch, where they were smothered and trampled to death, or more or less seriously injured.

The streets about the Khodynski Field disclosed horrible scenes. We passed wagons, filled partly with gifts for the populace and partly with corpses. Here and there, an arm, a leg or the head of an unhappy victim would protrude.

The most depressing thing was that we had to go to a ball on the evening of that fatal day, given at the French Embassy. For some inexplicable reason, it had not been called off. All other festivities attendant upon the Coronation were, of course, stopped, and on the next morning the Imperial Couple accompanied by General Neidhart made the rounds of all the hospitals, and visited and consoled the wounded. Witte, the Secretary of Finance, received Imperial orders not to spare Government funds to help and support the victims of this terrible catastrophe. Later, Goremykin, the Secretary of State, assured me, however, that the extent of the disaster had been exaggerated and that the casualties had not been as numerous as reported.

But the Tsar was not satisfied with this pacifying report, and ordered an investigation committee to be formed, under the chairmanship of Count Pahlen, the former Minister of Justice, a man renowned for his honor and fairness. But Count Pahlen had not reckoned with the pride of the Grand Dukes who declared that they would not tolerate a court of justice over them, and that rather than submit to such an indignity, they would lay down their Military and Government offices to demonstrate their displeasure.

The Grand Duchess Alexandra Yosefovna, a staunch upholder of ancient customs and tradition, spoke sharply to her relatives, and explained that opposition to the Tsar's orders was unworthy of a Russian nobleman, and added that, as it was, the Grand Dukes had no independent positions in the Empire, and whatever authority they possessed had been derived from the Emperor. She went so far—she told me later—as to indicate to the Grand Dukes, that similar insubordination in the days of Nicholas I would have been punished with exile to Siberia.

Finally the committee of investigation decided to let the Police Commissioner of Moscow bear the brunt of the Tsar's displeasure. He was dismissed. In the following year, Count Voronzov, the Secretary to the Court, also relinquished his post, and was replaced by the Baron, later Count Fredericks.

In June the Imperial couple went to Nizhni Novgorod, where a grand exhibition of Russian industries was being held. The Princess Galitzine had recovered in the meantime, so that my temporary attendance at Court was ended. Although I would have been greatly interested to visit the exhibit, I did not go to Nizhni Novgorod but journeyed directly to my own estate, where my son was to be married. The ceremony took place in my private chapel on June 30th, and after the young couple had left, I remained alone. After the strain of the past Winter's social events, I began to rest and lived leisurely among my peasants in the pastoral quiet of the country.

By this time the Tsar and his wife had started on their trip abroad, had had a meeting with the German Emperor and with the Emperor Francis Joseph of Austria, had gone to Denmark to visit the Tsar's grandfather, and to England to visit Queen Victoria, the Tsarina's grandmother. Then, via Cherbourg, they went to Paris. On their trip back to Russia, another unfortunate event marred their otherwise pleasant journey. Prince Lobanov, Secretary of Foreign Affairs, died suddenly in a compartment of the Imperial train.

Princess Helene Kochubei, Mistress of the Robes to the Empress Maria Fyodorovna

The Countesses Voronzov and Dashkov dressed as Court-Ladies in the days of Old-Russia

CHAPTER XVII

The Prison Problem—The Suicide of a Political Prisoner—Outrageous Attacks on Russia From Abroad—A Bitter Censure of the Inspector-General of Siberian Prisons—Unworthy Treatment of Prisoners—Aid—Money Through Count Ignatiev—The Intervention of the Tsar—Promotion of Our Work by the Administration.

I HAD BEEN neglecting my work on the Committee for Prison Care for some time, and decided to devote myself unsparingly to it again. The last international prison congress had been held in St. Petersburg in 1890, and as such a congress met every gve years the next one was imminent. In the meantime, an incident in the heart of Siberia had created a great deal of attention, and had caused the whole world to rise in hot indignation against Russian prison conditions.

It was the case of the woman Sigida, a political criminal, who had been imprisoned in the convict prison near Narshinsk, and who, by order of the Prison Director, had been flogged. The shame and indignity of this treatment had caused the woman to commit suicide by poison, and a number of other prisoners had made similar attempts in order to escape their lot.

The Russian anti-Government papers seized upon this subject at once, and published one article after another condemning the conditions in Siberia. Even the English illustrated newspapers flaunted front pages depicting scenes of maltreatment of the convicts, purporting to be everyday occurrences in Russia. Kennan, an American who had visited Siberia twice, published a series of articles about conditions prevailing in its prisons, and protest meetings were held in England and America against these "Russian atrocities."

There is no doubt that many of the reproaches heaped upon our Government were exaggerated, or that at least not everything had been truthfully represented, but unfortunately much of it *was* true, and the illustrated papers had reproduced the essential spirit of conditions as they really were.

Under the shadow of this scandal, the Foreign Commissions were on the verge of refusing to assemble the next congress in St. Petersburg, but in the end no change of plan was made. When the foreigners arrived an interesting prison exhibit was staged in the Michail Manège, and the Prince and Princess Oldenburg conducted the guests through the Palace in person. Naturally, I was deeply interested in this congress, at which some of the greatest men of the various countries represented were to be present. Beltrani-Scala, the Italian criminologist, and the Frenchman Herbette proved particularly brilliant in the discussion. B. F. Kamorski, Inspector-General of the Siberian convict prisons, also spoke during the public lectures conducted by the Foreign Commissions.

As I wanted to know the truth about the Sigida case, I invited Kamorski to pay me a private visit, in the course of which I learned the facts, which were both interesting and sad.

"Severity and justice," he said, "are the most important factors, and we have neither the one nor the other."

When I asked him how it was possible for this Sigida woman and her fellow-sufferers to have procured the poison, as they were supposed to be in solitary confinement, he answered: "Even the most important rules are ignored there. And the sentry itself does not hesitate to smuggle whatever they want into their cells, and in addition supply them with the latest news. This explains the surprising fact that the convicts in our prisons are better informed about existing political conditions than the police."

Then he told me the sad details of the Sigida case. The disorder had begun when one of the woman prisoners had been transferred to another prison, for which purpose she had been pulled from her cot in the middle of the night, rolled in a blanket, and to the accompaniment of sneers and rude laughter had been carted through the towns. This brutal procedure had aroused the revolt of the other inmates. The Sigida woman had asked to see the director of the prison and as he entered her cell she had thrown a plate of soup at his head.

This director was a former hussar of the guard and a drunkard as well, who knew nothing about the rules and regulations of his present office. Under a former law, this misdemeanor on the part of the prisoner called for corporal chastisement, but this law had been amended some time before so that it did not apply to women and old men any longer. Whether it was that the director did not know of this amendment, or whether he simply ignored it, the result was that he gave orders to have the woman flogged. This humiliation was more than she could bear, and she took her life.

Kamorski's story made a deep impression on me, and I decided forthwith to start a relief activity for the Siberian convicts. This was not so simple, however. It soon become evident that the founding of any local relief committees in the provincial towns of Siberia was utterly impossible. The population in those districts was composed partly of peasants and partly of gold miners. A middle class upon whom one could rely as aid in the relief work was as good as nonexistent. At Kamorski's suggestion, I decided to found a home for the children of convicts near the Katorga of Narshinsk. I lost no time in talking about this plan to the Grand Duchess Eugenia Maximilianovna, the Princess Baryatinski, and to other friends, and full of enthusiasm we threw ourselves into the task. Kamorski's advice, always at our disposal, helped us immensely.

Our first anxiety was the means of collecting funds. But an unexpected piece of good luck came our way and saved us a great deal of worry. At a Court ball, I happened to come across Count Ignatiev, and told him of our new work. After a few minutes of silence, he said he might be able to have some money at our disposal.

"When I was Minister of Finance," he said, "I used to be interested in the problems relating to exile to Siberia, and had collected a sum of money from various people for the promotion of a plan I had worked out in this connection. As I left the Ministry suddenly, my plan was never carried out. The money is, most likely, still lying in the safe of the Ministry office where I had placed it. Considering the fact that your efforts are concerned with the same kind of work I had planned, you may be able to get the use of these funds for your purpose."

It is not difficult to imagine how gladly I accepted this suggestion of Count Ignatiev's, which bade fair to place us in possession of a large sum of money. I wrote to the Assistant Secretary of Finance, Plehve, and begged him to call on me. When he came, I asked him if he knew anything about that money, and he answered that he knew all about it, as Count Ignatiev had spoken to him of it at the time, and about his Siberian project for which it had been collected. He said that he would make all the necessary inquiries and would do everything in his power to have the money assigned to me.

The money was indeed intact, but we had to obtain

Tsar Alexander III with his wife, Maria Fyodorovna and their children

The Princess Dolgoruky in the year 1867

the consent of the original donors before we could dispose of it. Some of them had died, so that many delays and difficulties arose before we had finally settled with the heirs. Count Ignatiev came to our assistance again and saw to it that everything was arranged in our favor as quickly as possible. Finally we obtained the consent of the Emperor.

I was elated and thanked the Emperor for his confidence in me; I also thanked Ignatiev, Durnovo and Plehve for their kindness and invaluable assistance. I now had a considerable sum of money at my disposal, as well as some real estate and buildings, and was ready to launch an undertaking which was soon to bear satisfactory fruit.

First of all, I wanted to know as much as possible about Siberian conditions, and for that purpose drove to see the Baroness Korff, wife of the Governor-General of Siberia. As soon as I explained what I wanted the Baroness was delighted to be able to help. It just happened, she said, that a Doctor Podubski had lately arrived in St. Petersburg; he knew Siberian conditions intimately, and was particularly well acquainted with those of the prison colony of Saghalin.

Dr. Podubski called, upon my invitation, and gave me a wealth of valuable information. Finally, he brought me a detailed report about Saghalin, which he had composed himself. At the same time he told me that, according to information he had received, a State Council meeting with the Emperor presiding was to be held within the next few days, and that the work of our committee was one of the items of the business of the day.

Under these circumstances, I thought it very important to give Dr. Podubski's pamphlet to the Emperor, but I did not know how to go about it. As the Empress was not in town, I decided to write to the Tsar, but just as I was composing the letter, it occurred to me that the approaching birthday of the Grand Duchess Maria Pavlovna might offer me an opportunity to speak to the Emperor directly.

On the following morning, therefore, I went to see the Grand Duchess at the Vladimir Palace, secretly hoping that the Tsar might also come to offer his congratulations. The air of excitement about the company corroborated my supposition, and I realized that the Emperor really was expected; but to my dismay I heard Baron Fredericks say, as he pointed to the clock, that the Tsar was late and presumably would only stay a few minutes.

I was afraid that I would have no chance to speak to him of my business, and was therefore somewhat discouraged when, as I greeted the Emperor and whispered almost inaudibly, "Your Majesty, I have something to tell you," he really seemed not to have heard my remark and continued his round of the room. But he returned to me and taking me over to a window, he asked:

"You have something to tell me? What is it?"

"I wanted to report to you about Saghalin, Your Majesty," I said.

"About Saghalin? I am very much interested," cried the Emperor.

I was delighted to tell him of our work and about Podubski's report, whereupon he asked me to send it to him within a week. This seemed to corroborate Podubski's information that a State Council meeting referring to our work was to be held within the next few days.

I hastened to the ladies of my committee, who were expecting me, and repeated my conversation with the Emperor, and asked them to prepare an abridged copy of Podubski's report for His Majesty. But contrary to my expectations my success with the Emperor was not received as jubilantly as I had expected. On the contrary, they exhibited dismay and disapproval. The ladies regretted that I had hurt our cause in my haste. For they were sure that the Ministers would never forgive my having approached the Emperor over their heads.

I tried to smooth over their objections and succeeded finally in placating their overwrought spirits. Then I wrote to the Minister of Justice and begged him to call on me. I told him everything, just as it had happened, and asked him how I was to report to the Tsar.

"You did well," he said. "And I can tell you, confidentially, that His Majesty expects to take up the prison question one of these days. As our official reports are very dry and wearisome, I am sure that His Majesty will utilize the clear and lively report you are sending him, as the basis on which he will make his decision."

And indeed, the result of that meeting was very favorable to our aims. The administration was ordered to promote our work as zealously as possible, and so we were well equipped to develop the constantly growing amount of relief work for the Siberian convicts. Our most important achievement became the nursery on the convict island of Saghalin, where the children of the exiles received the best care and treatment.

Some of the ladies of our committee expressed a wish to visit the Schlüsselburg Fortress at times, so that they might console the convicts with their kindly words. As I knew how difficult it would be to obtain such permission, I tried to speak to the Emperor in behalf of their intention, but he was not interested and I had to relinquish my plea at once. Yet this conversation with him, although negative in its result, was to prove useful later on, when some of the members of the Committee went to see the Secretary of State, Plehve, with the same request. They were then able to say that I had already informed the Tsar about the matter, so that Plehve undertook the task of submitting our request to the Emperor again, and this time he consented.

The ladies of the committee were now able to visit the Schlüsselburg Fortress, and when the prison administration realized that we were not pursuing any political object, they were more than agreeable to us. It was not until Plehve was murdered that these visits to the fortress were definitely forbidden to everyone, without exception!

CHAPTER XVIII

The Inclinations and Education of Nicholas II—His Indecision and Lack of Self-Confidence — The Empress and the Princesses of Montenegro—Visit to the Empress Frederick—A Conversation With Leo XIII—The Pope Objects to Materialism—Queen Margherita of Italy Fosters German Music—The Charlatan Dr. Philippe—Their Majesties Visit France—The Tsaritna and the Wife of the President—Problems of Etiquette—Offending the Mayor of Paris—The Empress's Hysterical Pregnancy.

DURING the period following the Coronation, I saw a good deal of the young Imperial couple. The Tsarina showed a lively interest in my prison relief work, and the Tsar liked to talk with me about episodes of his childhood days, with which I was better acquainted than most of the people about him. Altogether, our relationship was one of simple friendliness. Nicholas II, although his mother had always spoken with pleasure of his application to and interest in his studies, had remained a man with a small horizon and a narrow outlook, after all. He had grown up in the Anichkov Palace and for many years had hardly ever gone beyond its garden wall. Later, in Gachina, his life remained essentially unchanged except that the park was larger than the garden. He was fond of gymnastics, sports and exercise in the open air, but he had always been surrounded by the same atmosphere, and the same companions which had been chosen for him by the Tsarina, his mother. He wore his little sailor suits longer than most boys do, and his adolescence began comparatively late, and he developed slowly. Later, when he entered his Military service, he joined the other officers in a spirit of superficial comradeship, based on no mutual interests to bind him to them, with no desire for an exchange of opinions, and in fact with no difference of opinion at all. No one had uttered anything of importance in his presence; rather everyone invariably attempted to chat about trivial matters only.

As successor to the throne, and as Crown Prince, he had never taken the slightest interest in matters of government. Thus, at the age of twenty-six, he was placed at the helm of a gigantic empire. The only principle of which he was distinctly conscious, one which had been infused in his blood, was that of his absolute power. He had not the slightest knowledge of the revolutionary uprisings which had always been silently suppressed with a hand of iron. Yet, deplorable as this lack of preparation for rulership was, it could have yielded to enlightenment and knowledge had his wife been a better counsellor and had his political advisers been more experienced and more reliable.

I had often read and heard the criticism that Nicholas II had a "Janus Head." This reproach, however, was undeserved, nor did it properly describe his character. The fact was that he had no confidence in himself. He began to become aware of his lack of experience and education and for that reason could not issue an order without immediately beginning to doubt its wisdom, and revoking it, or if the latter course were impossible, he would be willing to compromise. Often a Minister of State would submit a report, and obtain the Tsar's consent to some measure or another, and within a few hours receive a letter from the Emperor in which the latter recanted everything.

The Empress had become very friendly with Anastasia Nikolayevna Leuchtenberg, a former Montenegrin Princess. The Tsarina was sorry for her and regarded her as a neglected wife because her husband spent most of his time abroad. And as her financial condition was in a state of disorder, the Empress not only consoled her in her loneliness, but also assisted her materially. But the strongest bond between these two women was their religious ecstasy. Their friendship was intensified when they were joined by Anastasia's older sister Militsa Nikolayevna, wife of the Grand Duke Peter Nikolayevich. Militsa was well versed in the mystic and occult sciences, and made the Empress acquainted with books on Indian philosophy, from her well-stocked library, which were to introduce the Empress to mysticism.

At that time the Empress Alexandra was completely well, enjoyed horseback riding, and once she gave the Emperor a surprise when, dressed in the uniform of her regiment, she reviewed a parade of a regiment of Uhlans. She often used to take walks with the Emperor to the Sergei Villa where Militsa lived. Besides, the ladies met every evening. As I was a frequent guest for luncheon in the small castle, I had occasion to notice how merry Their Majesties were.

My unsatisfactory state of health and the advice of my physician compelled me to go to Homburg. There I paid my respects to the Empress Frederick, who received me with the question:

"Are you related to the Princess Kurakin who was Court Lady to Mimi?" (The Tsarina Maria Fyodorovna.) She then spoke intimately about my mother, and we became better acquainted. Among other things, she observed:

"Mimi and I share the same sad fate, but she is happier than I am, for Nicky is charming to his mother."

The outstanding trait in the Empress Frederick's character was her self-love. She had waited with impatience for the end of her father-in-law, William I, but her husband had scarcely acceded to the throne when he became fatally ill of cancer, so that the Imperial crown slipped from her head before it could attain any power or influence for her. As soon as her son became Emperor, he made it his first task to refuse his mother the right of any interference in matters of Government; on the contrary, he suggested that it would be better for her to retire to her residence in Friedrichshof near Homburg. It was there that I called on her. She invited me to luncheon several times, and spoke of Queen Victoria's seventy-fifth anniversary which was to be celebrated that year, and also inquired about the details of the Coronation of the Tsarina Alexandra Fyodorovna. She impressed me as being an intelligent, cultured woman, but she seemed to feel the need of some definite aim in life. She hated Prince Bismarck, and regarded him as a personal enemy.

The following year, I took a cure at Karlsbad, and went from there to Rome, at which city I stopped in a hotel close by the home of my friends the Baryatinskis. Diplomats, well-known personages in Italian society, as well as Russians living in Rome, comprised the social circle of my friends. After the Parliamentary sessions, the Ministers would gather there in the evening, and one was always certain of hearing or participating in interesting and spirited conversations.

The year 1900 began in January with the Papal Jubilee, and Rome overflowed with visitors from all ends of the earth, who had come to congratulate His Holiness, Leo XIII. This old man, in the course of whose lifetime so many important events had happened, was carried out of the Vatican on his Seggio Pontificale. Facing the people, he rose from his seat, and blessed them. The enthusiasm of the populace was indescribable. Everyone

Tsar Nicolai as Crown Prince and the Grand Duchess Elizabeth at a Costume Ball

The Church of the Saviour in Moscow on March 1, 1881

shouted, wept, waved, and sometimes one could even hear cries of "Viva il Papa Re!"

After the festivities had terminated, I had an audience with the Pope. The officiating Abbate conducted me into the room and disappeared. Leo XIII sat on a great red chair like a throne. I approached and kissed his hand. He pointed to a small tabouret covered with red velvet, and asked me to be seated. Then he began to converse, first in Italian, soon however dropping into French, and thereby making the conversation much easier for me.

He began by voicing his satisfaction at the diplomatic relations between Russia and Rome, brought about in Vienna by Prince Lobanov, and Cardinal Rampolla. Then he begged me to convey his good wishes to the Tsar, and his desire for the former's support of peace with Poland. He then discoursed on materialism and its danger to all mankind, and said he thought all Christians should oppose it in a body; he dwelt on this subject in lively, colorful words. Finally he gave me a message to the Emperor, assuring him of his support.

In appearance the Pope was thin and pale, so that one involuntarily thought of an alabaster lamp in which a flame was burning. This flame radiated from his eyes which sparkled like black carbuncles. His speech was rapid, his gestures of Italian liveliness; he chose his words discreetly, and exhibited wisdom in his every remark.

I also had an audience with Queen Margherita, and found her to be a very cultured woman, and patroness of all scientific, literary and artistic enterprises. She was deeply interested in German music and had tried with enthusiasm to make it popular in Italy; her Friday evening musicales were devoted to that purpose. She knew that I was engaged in prison relief work, and asked many intelligent questions on the subject, as well as about Russia in general, which she had visited a few years before.

In the fall of 1900, the Tsar fell dangerously ill of typhus in the Crimea; the Tsarina nursed him day and night, as devotedly and efficiently as a professional nurse, although as an expectant mother she needed care herself. For some time the Emperor's condition seemed very serious, so that the Ministry of State had to prepare for the possibility of his death. It was decided to name the Grand Duke Michael Alexandrovich successor to the throne, but not until the expected Imperial child was born. The Empress, an affectionate wife and in her delicate condition, was profoundly hurt and shocked by these considerations. Fortunately, all this anxiety proved unnecessary when the danger had passed.

At about this time the son of the Court Commandant, Hesse, had also fallen ill. Militsa Nikolayevna was anxious about this boy, and also about the Emperor, and exaggerated the illness of both patients. She constantly spoke about her friend, the wonder-doctor, Philippe, whose prayers alone could cure the sick. This Philippe, as a matter of fact, was no physician at all. On the contrary, the French Academy of Medicine regarded him as a charlatan. He lived in Lyons, where he was engaged in all sorts of spiritualistic and occult experiments. Besides all this, he was a Freemason.

That Winter, when the son of Anastasia Nikolayevna also became ill, Philippe was summoned to St. Petersburg to treat him. The young man lived in private quarters in the Galernaya, and it was there that Philippe met the Imperial couple, who had come to visit the patient.

I was very much surprised to receive a telegram from the Princess Galitzine, asking me to come to Dunkirk. I had read in the newspapers that the Emperor had gone to Kiel to witness the naval manoeuvres there, and that, in order not to make France uneasy, he had also consented to be present at the French manoeuvres at Compiègne. I would never have suspected that the Empress would accompany her husband on this trip, and as a matter of fact I thought it undesirable for several reasons. But she could not make up her mind to let him go alone. Several embarrassing situations might have been avoided had she refrained from this journey.

We spent a good deal of time discussing what the Empress's attitude toward the wife of the French President, Loubet, ought to be. As the wife of the head of the French Republic, Madame Loubet had a claim to every honor due a hostess, but I knew the Tsarina sufficiently to foresee difficulties in that quarter. As soon as we arrived at Paris, I read the announcements of the arrival of our Emperor and his consort, and about the preparations for their reception. I met Prince Urussov and asked him what the program of the reception was, but he declared he knew of nothing in that connection beside the visit to Compiègne, which was of a purely military character. He added that the presence of the Tsarina had changed the whole arrangement.

"Let us hope that she may be agreeable," he said.

And then he told me that the Tsar had asked the favor of having the title of Doctor conferred upon some charlatan by the name of Philippe, and that the French Academy of Medicine had felt insulted and had brusquely refused to do this. I was alarmed by this report, and profoundly regretted that the Tsar had compromised his authority by this tactless move.

On the appointed day the steamer *La France,* aboard which was the French President and some of the higher officers, came to greet their foreign guests. It had been suggested that I accompany them, but I preferred to await the arrival of Their Majesties at the dock. Count Lambsdorff, our Secretary of Foreign Affairs, presented M. Delcassé, who held the same post in France, and who had engineered this very event. The weather was so stormy that the President and his suite were unable to board the Russian steamer, and had to be content to escort their guests. After the usual presentations, we attended a gala luncheon at which I found myself seated next to the French Minister of Justice, M. Monis. We both recalled that it was in this very place, Dunkirk, that a Tsar had visited for the first time in history. This was Peter the Great, who had come here accompanied by my ancestor, Prince Kurakin.

After luncheon we took the train to Compiègne. The Empress was fatigued. Her face was flushed and she complained of a headache. At the first opportunity, I approached her and told her that she was expected in Paris, and that if she disappointed the Parisians, it would amount to a grave offense and give cause to all kinds of rumors. But she replied:

"No, no. We have been in Paris already. This time we have only come to witness the manoeuvres, et puis, il ya toujours l'histoire de l'argent, qui est si désagréable."

I think she was referring to the loan which Russia was intending to make in France, and she was afraid that the French might regard her visit in the light of an importunity. And she stubbornly clung to this obsession.

A carriage in which she, myself and two ladies of honor took our seats, awaited the Tsarina in Compiègne. The Emperor together with the President had preceded us. Our coach followed theirs, and behind us came the whole suite. Darkness was beginning to fall. Here and there a fire would flare up. The military band played

The Grand Dukes Alexander and Vladimir Alexandrovich

The Grand Duke Sergei Antonovich as Tsaryevich Fydor at an an
performance of Tolstoy's "Boris Godunov"

our national hymn and Le Marseillaise, alternately, and the populace shouted:

"Vive la Russie! Vive la France!"

At seven o'clock the following morning, we drove to the manoeuvres. The road lay between wide fields and along the side stood people on horseback and on foot or seated in their wagons. The enthusiasm was great. They shouted, "Vive la Russie! Vive la France! Vive la Tsarine!" and a number of times, even: "Vive la dame à la gauche!" which was meant for me. I have often since laughed at that original salutation.

Late in the evening, tired out from the impressions of the day and the fresh air, we returned to Compiègne. These excursions were repeated daily in the same routine. The thought that we had seen Madame Loubet for only a few minutes troubled me, and I was wishing that the Empress had asked the President's wife to accompany her on her drive to the manoeuvres instead of myself, just once. One day had been reserved, very likely to give us a chance to visit Paris; then, only was I commissioned to invite Madame Loubet in the name of the Empress.

Next morning, M. Doucat, the Mayor of Paris, came to Compiègne to invite the Tsar to the capital, where extensive preparations for his arrival had already been begun. I don't know to this day why Waldeck Rousseau had persuaded Count Lambsdorff to refuse this invitation; perhaps he and his party wanted to receive the Emperor alone. At any rate the Tsar was not told of M. Doucat's call. He was very much perturbed, when he was informed of this faux pas, later, and made use of the next opportunity to greet Doucat and express his regret that "this time" it had not been possible for him to visit Paris. However, the embarrassment, and the affront to the Parisians, could not be undone.

On the day before the Grand Military Parade, President Loubet gave a gala dinner, followed by a rout. At table, Their Majesties sat in the middle, with M. Loubet next to the Tsarina, and Madame Loubet next to the Tsar. I sat directly opposite them, between Waldeck-Rousseau and Fallières. While our conversation was animated and very interesting to me, I could not help glancing across the table repeatedly. What I saw did not look well. The conversation between the Emperor and Madame Loubet was just as jejune as that between the Empress and the President.

The parade on the following morning presented an imposing spectacle. The Tsar was on horseback; the Empress drove in the carriage with me, as did the President with Waldeck-Rousseau and Fallières. Another formal luncheon took place after the parade, during which I had a talk with Cardinal Lavigerie. I told him about Rome and my audience with the Pope.

The hour came for our train to roll into the station, and we left France, escorted as far as the border by the French gentlemen. The Emperor was in high spirits, and expressed his conviction that France would revert to a monarchy some day, as the people seemed to have treated the sovereigns with great deference and respect. I did not agree with him, and told him that in my opinion this would never happen. It was the Republic which protected them against the intrigues of the three monarchistic parties, the Legitimists, the Orelans, and the Bonapartists. Besides, I felt that the Republic suited the people best.

We journeyed from there to Kiel, where the Imperial children were staying under the care of the Princess Irene, and were received by Prince Henry of Prussia, and his wife the sister of our Tsarina. From Kiel we went to Poland, where Their Majesties intended to spend the autumn in Skiernewicze. I left the Imperial train at a wayside station, and traveling via Moscow, went home where my family was impatiently awaiting my return.

Throughout our entire trip across the fields of Compiègne, the Empress had not once mentioned the name of Doctor Philippe, but I knew that in her thoughts and prayers she sought contact with him. She regarded him as the guardian of her beloved husband. It was natural that her mood even outwardly expressed itself, so that her absent-mindedness was interpreted by the French as frigidity, pride and lack of charm. This impression became even more pronounced by reason of the contrast presented by Their Italian Majesties when they visited France a short time later. The Italian Queen was simple and charming, particularly to Madame Loubet, and she left the most pleasant impression with the Parisians.

In the Spring of 1902, President Loubet came to Tsarskoye Selo, to return the Emperor's visit. I would have liked to be present at the reception, but I suddenly fell ill and passed through a critical siege. However, while still in bed I received a lovely enameled vase which had been sent to me by M. Loubet.

When I had recovered sufficiently to stand the exertion, I went to my country estate, and awaited a telegram from the Princess Galitzine, which would inform me of the birth of the child the Tsarina was expecting. My astonishment was surely great, when I received the following letter from her:

"Dear Friend, do not come. There will be no christening—there is no child—there is nothing! It is a catastrophe!"

It developed that the Empress had believed herself pregnant only because of the suggestion of Philippe. She had refused to consult any physician until the normal period of pregnancy had passed. It was only then that it became possible to ascertain that the whole unfortunate episode was the result of a severe nervous disturbance.

It just happened that a great many foreign guests were gathered in St. Petersburg at the time, to attend the wedding of the Grand Duchess Elena Vladimirovna to the Greek Prince. A grand performance had been arranged at the theatre just on this critical day, and despite his nervousness and agony, the Emperor was forced to put in his appearance in the centre box. He was deathly pale, as he went through the ordeal of answering all the inquiries concerning the Tsarina's health. As soon as the curtain had fallen on the last scene, he left the theatre to go to Znamenskoye, where Philippe was staying. I don't know how the charlatan managed to extricate himself from the situation. At any rate, nothing serious happened to him, although he deserved to be severely dealt with.

CHAPTER XIX

The Fatal Prophecies of Dr. Philippe—Danger of War—No One Wants War But Everyone Helps to Bring It About—The Stubbornness of the Empress—Sojourn In Italy and France—A Conversation With the Empress-Mother—The Tsaritna Is Offended—My Act of Mediation—Birth of the Crown Prince—The Unpopular War—Insufficient Military Preparation—The Battle of Chuchema.

In the beginning of the Summer, I received a letter from the Princess Galitzine, in which she informed me that the Empress had inquired for me several times. Besides, there was a message from the Tsarina herself, to the effect that there was an apartment ready for me in the Peterhof. Accordingly I left my estate and went to the Capital directly after this amiable invitation, and paid my respects to the Empress.

I found her and the whole Court in a state of great excitement over various stupid rumors which had been spread about her. No one at that time could foresee what proportions this organized baiting of the Empress would assume a decade later, and to what a disastrous end it would lead. Measured by the monstrous calumnies of later years, the censure of the Empress at the time was comparatively harmless, but sufficient to throw her into a state of hysteria.

I remained in Peterhof for about a month, until their Majesties left for Spala. Then I left for Florence, where I was to be a guest at the Baryatinski villa. At about the same time, Dr. Philippe disappeared from St. Petersburg, but his spirit continued to rule at the Tsar's Court. He had always prophesied that Russia was chosen to dominate the whole East, and I do not believe I am exaggerating when I claim that these prophecies of the charlatan were in no small measure responsible for the fatal turn taken by Russian politics in the East.

The Japanese were still trying to effect a friendly agreement with us and the Mikado had sent the Marquis Ito to St. Petersburg, for the purpose of forming an alliance between Japan and Russia. But Ito had been so coldly and ungraciously received there, that he left for England at once, where he was enthusiastically greeted. The result of these affronts was an English-Japanese alliance, directed against us.

Count Lambsdorff, at that time the leader of our foreign politics, was a man who had spent his entire term of service in the office of the Ministry, and one who knew the traditions of Russian politics accurately. He was an outspoken opponent of a Russo-Chinese alliance, and had sent in his resignation a number of times, whenever the Emperor had made any decision regarding foreign politics over his head. Another factor, not entirely without its effect on the course of events, was the counsel of William II of Germany, who constantly issued warnings about the "Yellow Peril," and who seemed to be trying to push Russia in a more and more Easterly direction.

It must be stated, however, that all our statesmen fought against the idea of a war with Japan and that they repeatedly demonstrated the uselessness of such a step to the Emperor. The Tsar himself continued to declare that in no case would the situation result in a conflict, as he did not desire war. Yet everything was done in Russia to make this catastrophe inevitable. Consequently it was not surprising that in 1904 the Japanese Ambassador severed his diplomatic relations with us in the name of his Government and asked for his papers.

I had been absent from Court throughout this period,

as my unsteady health compelled me to rest. At the beginning of 1902, I had returned from Italy and had begun to take up my work, when I suffered a serious attack of pneumonia. The Tsarina visited me during this illness and brought me, among other things, a gold medallion with the picture of Seraphim of Sarov, the miracle worker, for whose canonization she was diligently working at that time.

She was persistent in the matter, and would listen to no objections. When she was told that certain difficulties of an ecclesiastical nature demanded at least a delay of the canonization, she answered simply that the Emperor's wish would suffice to remove any such obstacle instantly. According to her, Seraphim received the greatest love and reverence among the Russian people, and his canonization would be received with unanimous sympathy. The poor Tsarina did not know of the phrase that was making the rounds in Society: "It would be difficult to know where Philippe ends and Seraphim begins."

In the fall of 1903, I had to leave Russia again in order to recuperate at the Riviera, and so I went to Beaulieu, between Mentone and Nizza, where I took long drives in the automobile of my friend Polovzev. We often drove to Cannes, where many of my acquaintances were stopping. Among these was the Grand Duchess Maria Alexandrovna, accompanied by the Countess Alexandra Andreyevna Tolstoy.

With the approach of Spring, I went to Paris in order to consult some physicians there, and took the occasion to call on Madame Loubet, the wife of the President of France; there I also met the future French Ambassador to Russia, M. Bompar, and his wife who had just arrived from Madagascar. The Bompars were vastly different from Monsieur and Madame Loubet, who had so far represented their Government in Russia. M.

Bompar was intelligent and well read and a Republican by conviction, who was neither adroit in the art of social conversation nor familiar with the finesse of Court etiquette. Consequently he was not seldom guilty of an offense against the formalities, thus arousing derision and unfavorable criticism against himself. His wife was amiable and sympathetic, but endowed with no special qualities whereby she might attract the admiration of our St. Petersburg society. I could foresee that they would meet with many a difficulty, and made up my mind to assist them to the best of my ability.

In Vichy, where I had gone to take the after-cure, I learned about the uprising in Serbia, about the murder of King Alexander and his wife, and about Peter Karageorgevich's accession to the throne. All this made me anxious, and I wondered if these events did not imply the danger of war, as unrest in the Balkans had so often done before. However, this affair was amicably settled by our Emperor's recognition of King Peter.

I returned to Russia that summer, and arrived just in time for the canonization of Seraphim of Sarov, which ceremony was attended by the Emperor, his mother, the Empress, her children and the two Montenegrin Grand Duchesses. Shortly after, I had another attack of pneumonia, which confined me to my bed the entire winter, and several times I was on the brink of death.

Shortly after the outbreak of the Japanese war, I paid my respects to the Empress-Mother Maria Fyodorovna. She asked me whether I had seen her daughter-in-law. I answered:

"Yes, Madame, the Empress was so gracious as to call on me during my illness."

"How did you find her?"

"Remarkably fresh-looking, considering the excitement of the war."

"More than fresh, it seems," replied Maria Fyodorovna, with a tone of bitterness in her voice. "She is actually over-excited and full of enthusiasm."

I could see that the Empress-Mother by no means shared the mood of her daughter-in-law, and that she disapproved with all her heart of the conflict into which the nation had slipped. Several times during that talk with me, tears came to her eyes.

On the other hand, I knew the Tsarina well enough to understand why the war transported her into such enthusiasm. It was because she still believed in the prophecies of Philippe, and expected a marvelous triumph for Russia. Under his hypnotic influence, she had become blind to actual military and political conditions.

She passionately desired to assist in the Red Cross relief work, and had equipped some of the rooms in the Winter Palace with stores of linen and bandages. She used to come in every day, accompanied by her negro, and work diligently with the other ladies of the Red Cross.

In the Spring she called on me again and when she saw that my recovery was not making any marked progress, she invited me to move to Tsarskoye Selo with her, and enjoy the good air there. I was glad to accept, and found a large, beautiful room ready for me in the castle, in which I soon began to feel at home. The Tsarina came to see me frequently, and showed me the most touching attention on every occasion.

One morning she asked me to come to her, and I found her dissolved in tears. Indignantly she told me that when she had expressed to Count Voronzov her wish to display a greater activity in the Red Cross, he had coldly answered that the Red Cross was under the supervision of the Empress Maria Fyodorovna, and that outsiders could not proceed independently.

"Think of it," sobbed the Empress, "he called me an outsider! I would have like to tell him that he was forgetting the fact that he was speaking to his Empress!"

I told her that after all, Count Voronzov was not altogether wrong, as the Red Cross was an international society, in which the Empress would mean no more than any other member. However, I thought it might easily be possible to obtain a substation under the leadership of the Empress Maria Fyodorovna.

She took up this idea at once, and thought that in such a case she would take over the district of Kharbinsk.

"I don't dare to ask this of my mother-in-law, but I would be glad if you would drive to her, and talk things over with her. You may telephone right this moment and find out when you may see her."

The telephone was in the same room, and while I spoke to the officiating Chamberlain, the Empress stood behind me and told me—still sobbing—further details of the incident which had so upset her.

The Chamberlain informed me that the Empress-Mother was busy all day, but asked me to come to dinner. A few minutes later, I was called to the phone. It was Gachina calling, again, and Maria Fyodorovna was inviting me to spend the night there and return to Tsarskoye Selo with her the next morning.

Not without some trepidation, I started on my mission, for the information I had from the Tsarina was too confused to let me understand clearly what it was all about. Therefore, before I left Tsarskoye Selo I consulted Madame Geringer and asked her for detailed directions, which she was good enough to give me.

I arrived in Gachina an hour before dinner and had thus enough time to explain the Tsarina's wishes to the

Empress-Mother. Maria Fyodorovna consented at once and with pleasure, and thought it might well be possible to organize an independent branch of the Red Cross.

"She has splendid ideas," said Maria Fyodorovna of her daughter-in-law. "But she never tells me what she does or expects to do. When we two are together, she always converses about everything but herself. I shall be very glad if she will only drop her reserve."

Somewhat astonished, I answered:

"Pardon me, Madame, but these are the very words the Empress used. She regrets no less speaking with you only on indifferent topics, and would be happy if you would let her help you with the work."

"I should wish nothing better," was the Empress-Mother's answer. "But it is very difficult to understand her."

The Grand Duke Alexander Michailovich and the Grand Duchess Xenia Alexandrovna awaited us in the dining-room, and we sat together chatting pleasantly until midnight. All evening the Empress Mother had been very affectionate and kind to me. On the following morning we drove to Tsarskoye Selo in order to celebrate the Emperor's birthday by a service in church. The Emperor was not present himself. He was in the South just then, reviewing the troops on their way to the battle-front.

The Empress was expecting another child at that time, and so after I had returned to my country estate after a lengthy sojourn in Tsarskoye Selo, I again expected a telegram from the Princess Galitzine as I had two years before. This time one arrived with the happy news that a boy child had been born to the Empress, news which excited the inhabitants of our village to the highest pitch. The telegraph clerk had not been able to keep the official secret and the news had spread through the district like wildfire. Peasants from distant settlements came to me and inquired if it were really true that Russia now had a Tsaryevich.

I would gladly have gone to St. Petersburg to attend the baptism, knowing how happy the parents were over the birth of the boy. But my physical condition forbade the exertion of the trip and consequently I did not go to St. Petersburg till some time later.

I found the baby, a pretty, healthy boy, on a blue satin cover, edged with lace, lying on the Empress's chaise longue. As I bent down to kiss him, the Empress stood behind me, looking radiantly beautiful in the overbrimming happiness of a young mother.

The sovereigns' happiness stood in sharp contrast, however, to the prevailing mood of the nation. No one understood the war; no one, with the exception of the revolutionary party, had wanted it. They secretly expected from its outcome, a weakening of the Tsaristic regime.

Among the intelligentsia there were many who could rightfully have been called "Russian Japanese," so strong was their sympathy with our enemy. The people at large, too, saw nothing else in the war than the additional burdens it thrust upon them, and could not understand why it was necessary. A Russian recognizes a war only when it is in defense of his country, and will not approve of an offensive type of warfare. Why, he asks himself, should we sacrifice life and property in order that a distant, foreign people, of whom we have never heard before, may be conquered?

As a final straw, it was discovered that the military administration which had constantly been urging war, had neglected to prepare for it. The Army was not even provided with the indispensable mountain artillery, although appropriations had long ago been made for it;

and these were found to be still reposing in the Government banks. The fortifications at Port Arthur were in a pitiful condition; the number of regiments stationed in Siberia was insufficient; and the transportation of troops from Western Russia had only begun.

Krapotkin, the former Minister of War, was made Commander of the Army, and thus by a species of poetic justice was placed in a position to taste the consequences of his own negligence. The fleet was in command of Admiral Makarov, a seasoned commander of whom great things were expected. Misfortune dogged Russia's footsteps here as well, however, by the explosion of a mine which blew up the "Petropavlovsk" and destroyed the Admiral and with him our hopes.

Now all eyes were turned on General Kondratenko, who commanded the defense of Port Arthur. Our hopes centered on his holding the fortress until the arrival of the Baltic fleet. But while Roshdestvenski's squadron was battling with countless obstacles, General Kondratenko, too, was killed. Even then, many Russians regarded the war as lost.

On the day of the battle of Chuchema, I happened to be in the Palace where the anniversary of the Coronation was being celebrated, and took this opportunity to ask the Tsar if he had had any news about the fleet.

"So far I have heard nothing," he said, "but I expect a report any minute."

And with characteristic optimism, he added:

"Let's hope that no news is good news."

But on the next morning, in Gachina, Alexander Michailovich showed me a copy of the report in which Admiral Togo informed his Mikado of the complete destruction of the Russian fleet.

CHAPTER XX

In Italy Again—Echoes of Russian Events In Rome—I Visit Queen Margherita and Queen Elena—The Wanderings of Our Nursery—The Tsar and Count Witte—The Freedom of the Press and Its Consequences—Anna Vyrubova and Her Husband — Orlov, the Constant Traveling Companion of the Tsarina—The Opening of the Duma—Stolypin Becomes Prime Minister—Rasputin's First Appearance at Court.

IN THE beginning of 1905 I went to Italy again, as the doctors had insisted that I spend the Winter in the South. My friend Baryatinski had again asked me to visit her in her Roman Palazzo, and so late in the Fall of 1904 I left Russia and went South. After a protracted sojourn in Florence I arrived safely at Rome, where I presently found myself in the midst of a large circle of pleasant and interesting people.

Conversation, naturally, always reverted to the subject of the war, and I was compelled to make the painful discovery that the Italians, despite their social tact, could not refrain from giving the impression that they looked down upon Russia and her attitude with a kind of pitying censure. I saw that they regarded us as a nation which had already lost its standing as a great European Power. That this grave point of view with regard to the events that had taken place was not entirely groundless became apparent shortly when reports were received of the "bloody Sunday" in St. Petersburg and the ominous days following it. The Roman newspapers all wrote about the Russian Revolution and the imminent overthrow of the Tsaristic Government. Photographs of the dead and wounded victims of the "bloodthirsty Russian regiment of terror" were sold everywhere.

To add to this, in February the Grand Duke Sergei Alexandrovich, the brother-in-law of the Empress, was killed by a bomb in Moscow, an act of violence which had a profound effect on all minds. It was regarded as a sure sign of the approaching collapse of the Imperial Power! All this depressed me to such a degree that I disliked to go out among people, but I considered it my duty to pay my respects to the Italian Court.

When the Queen Mother, Margherita, heard that I was visiting in Rome she sent me an invitation, which I gladly accepted. After the death of her husband she had moved from the Quirinal, leaving it to her son, Victor Emmanuel II, and had gone to live in a new Palace specially built for her. I found her just as attractive as before, and still as warmly interested in all problems of culture, music, poetry and science. Our talk drifted to the tragic episode at Moscow, and she could not get over the fact that the Grand Duchess Elizabeth had visited the assassin of her husband in prison.

"I shall never be able to understand what made her do it," she cried, as she covered her face with her hands.

However, I thought I noticed a certain reserve about the Queen whenever Russia was mentioned, and got the impression that her sympathies in the conflict were on the Japanese side. Naturally, she was too tactful to express herself one way or another, but some of her remarks displayed her attitude clearly enough.

As I had visited the Queen Mother, propriety demanded that I be presented to the Young Queen, Elena, as well. She, too, was a fascinating and charming person, and like her mother-in-law kept a great hospitable house. When she conversed with me she used the Russian language, and entertained me with many recollections and reminiscences from the time when she was still an insignificant Montenegrin Princess at the Smolni Institute.

In the meantime, the Japanese had taken the island of Saghalin, which made me very anxious about our nursery there. Fortunately, my fears were quickly dispelled by a report from St. Petersburg to the effect that the Japanese had transferred our little colony to Yokohama, and thence across the Pacific back to Odessa. I found out later that the Japanese children had been most amiable to the little Russian exiles, while en route through Japan, and had cheered them with generous gifts of toys. At my request the transport was met in Odessa by General Neidhart, who saw to it that the children were supplied with food and clothing and were sent on to Moscow.

Soon after, the official negotiations for peace with Japan were begun. They were conducted on the Russian side by Sergey Julievich Witte. This man justified the Emperor's confidence in him beyond all expectations, and conducted the affair so masterfully that in the end, the conditions of peace proved much more favorable than had been generally expected.

However, there existed a strange relationship between the Emperor and Witte. The former was forced to appreciate the diplomat's great talent, his adroitness and his extensive education, but he never could trust him completely. The vehemence with which Witte was in the habit of stating his opinions, embarrassed the Tsar. Perhaps he secretly feared that this clever and ambitious man might harbor dangerous plans for his own overthrow.

The Americans had approached Witte, or so it was rumored, and impressed him with the idea that the United States could profitably ally themselves with a republican and democratic Russia, and that thus united, the two nations could rule the whole world. Whether the Emperor believed such rumors or not, he nevertheless

The Grand Duke Paul as "Prince Christian"

Tsar Nicolai II and his wife Alexandra Fyodorovna

continued to distrust the newly made Count, and after having made every possible use of his talents, tried his best to remove him from the political scene as quickly as possible.

But peace conditions had not been reached rapidly enough to prevent another open outbreak which manifested the inner unrest. Just as I was returning to Russia from Italy, the railway and postal employees had gone on strike, and we were just fortunate enough to catch the last train back to St. Petersburg. The general ferment had grown to such dimensions that the Grand Duke Nicholai Nikolayevich was thrown into a state of panic, and in this mood joined Witte in the opinion that the outbreak of a revolution could be prevented only by the granting of constitutional reforms. Together with Witte, Nicolai Nikolayevich drew up the first draft of a constitution, and submitted it to the Emperor, declaring that he was carrying a pistol, and that if the Emperor refused to sign it, he would shoot himself on leaving the palace.

After protracted negotiations, a commission which was to work out the necessary reforms was created, with Alexander Grigoryevich as its president. Under pressure of the critical situation, the Tsar was compelled to name Count Witte Prime Minister, and the first act of the newly appointed dignitary was to give the power of freedom to the press. The newspapers made immediate use of their liberty, and printed daring jokes and caricatures, such as no other country in the world would have tolerated.

My indignation at all this was great. One day, when I happened to be seated next to the Minister of War at a luncheon in the Palace, I expressed my astonishment at the indulgence of the Government in regard to these publications.

"I am a military man," he answered, "and know nothing about political affairs, but I have been told that these very transgressions convict the newspapers, and prove the impossibility of having an unbridled press."

I replied that in my opinion, such an experiment was certainly dangerous, since poison remained poison, and no one could foresee the ravages which could be caused by this unparalleled campaign of baiting instituted by a liberal press.

It was at about this time that the marriage of Anna Taneyev to the naval lieutenant Vyrubov took place. She was the Anna Taneyev who later became so notorious at court. I had known her for years, and had always found her a simple, sweet, but somewhat over-excited girl. After she had recovered from a severe siege of typhus, her already manifested enthusiasm for the Empress had developed into a mania, and had assumed the aspect of a mystic superstition. Having been sent abroad to recuperate from her illness, she returned and began to adore the Empress in a passionate manner, and sought every opportunity to attract her attention. At first, the Empress was somewhat startled by the extravagant manner of the young girl, but gradually she began to pity Anna, as the young girl confided in her the difficulties of living with her family, and how little understanding she found in their midst. The falsity of these statements might have been unintentional, but they were far from true nevertheless, for I had rarely, if ever, known such devoted parents as those of Anna Taneyev.

After the War, Vyrubov, a naval lieutenant and cousin of Olenina, the Lady of Honor, appeared in St. Petersburg. He seemed not uninteresting to me in those days, especially when he told of his numerous experiences, which he did in a very animated way. He had been in the battle of Chuchema, and together with a sailor had been rather miraculously saved from drowning. He soon began to court Anna, but as she promptly refused him, he went to visit his brother in the country. Upon the latter's advice, and because he really loved Anna, he returned to St. Petersburg and proposed to her again. This time she accepted, and announced her engagement to him. I never could understand what had persuaded her to take this step, for apparently she had never felt the slightest affection for him.

The wedding took place in the big church of Tsarskoye Selo and was celebrated in the most sumptuous manner. The Empress wept bitterly, and her daughters, seeing their mother so profoundly moved, did the same. The young couple left, and on their return found that their villa had been decorated by the Tsarina herself. From that moment on, everything remained as before Anna's marriage. Early in the morning, the Empress would send for Anna and both remained inseparable during the day. Lieutenant Vyrubov would go to Kronstadt, where his official duties demanded his presence for a few hours daily, and the rest of the day he would roam about aimlessly. . . .

It was only natural that in the course of time this condition became intolerable. One evening the storm broke and in a violent scene he upbraided his wife for her neglect of him and her perfect disregard of any sort of domestic life. Its immediate consequence was that Anna went back to her parents, and declined to have any further discussions with her husband. Nor would her father receive his son-in-law any longer. His letters were returned unopened. Presently rumors began to circulate that Vyrubov had lost his reason in consequence of his excitement at the battle of Chuchima. The Secretary of the Court finally summoned him, and suggested that he consent to a divorce from Anna and incidentally intimated that this was the Emperor's wish.

The unhappy Vyrubov was very much grieved; in fact he wept, but gradually began to realize that a happy life with Anna had become impossible and so decided to release her from the ties which bound her to him. From that moment on, he disappeared from Court society. He married again and became the father of two children, but died a few years later. Anna, however, fell more and more under the Tsarina's influence. The latter finally took Anna to live with her and supported her financially.

Among those who accompanied the Imperial family on their frequent trips to the Skerries, one Orlov, the Commander of Her Majesty's regiment of Uhlans, held a special position. Evil gossip was gradually spread regarding his relations with the Tsarina, for Orlov, a good-looking officer and a famous man-about-town, had charming and elegant manners, and pleased both Their Majesties probably as much because of his personal elegance as by his unconditional devotion to them, which he proved by his punitive expedition against the revolutionary Lettish Barones. The Tsarina was very proud of her regiment, and what could be more natural than for its commander to become persona grata at Court?

I will admit that the Empress flirted with him a little, and that such an indiscretion on the part of a woman ordinarily as cold and proud as she, was bound to attract considerable attention. But despite all this, I am absolutely convinced that nothing passed between these two, that she with her high code of morals would not be able to have justified. When Orlov participated in a trip to the Skerries for the last time, he was already seriously ill with consumption. His mode of living had done much to undermine his already weakened system; as a matter of fact, he was supposed to go to Egypt, but had preferred to accept the Tsarina's invitation. Soon, however, his condition became so alarming that he had to leave the Imperial yacht and go to his children in Tsarskoye Selo, where he died shortly after. I was present at his funeral, in the company of the Imperial family, and witnessed how the Emperor helped to carry the coffin to the grave after the funeral mass.

In the meantime, the Bulygin Commission had finished its work. Continuous meetings under the chairmanship of the Emperor would now take place in the Palace in Peterhof, in which the laws governing the future relationship of the Tsar to the Duma were to be settled, on the basis of the material submitted. These negotiations tormented the Emperor very much. A few years later, when we happened to be in the Hall of the Portraits in Peterhof, he said:

"This place reminds me of evil days. I felt all the time that this person (Witte) was trying to lead me onto a wrong path, but I had not enough strength to oppose him."

Finally, in April, the first Duma was opened. The Imperial family, together with all high Military and Civil officers and the Court ladies had gathered in the cathedral of the Winter Palace *en grande toilette,* and wearing all their jewels. Opposite us stood the deputies with triumphant expressions. The Empress Alexandra looked depressed; Maria Fyodorovna, serious as always. We were conducted to the throne, the doors opened and the Emperor entered. He was a dignified figure as he walked through the long hall. Stopping before the throne, he delivered his speech, in a loud, amiable and clear voice, addressing the Deputies as "beloved people." A loud hurrah greeted him in return. The tears rose to my eyes, and the Princess Galitzine told me afterwards, that at that moment she had the feeling that something great was crashing—as if all Russian tradition had been annihilated by a single blow.

The Deputies, who were being carried on a steamer down the Neva to the Tauric Palace, gave a naive expression to their enthusiasm. They raised a red flag, sang revolutionary songs, jeered at the past in their speeches, and never thought of thanking the Emperor, who had just sacrificed so many precious traditions to them. Everyone thought of the battle. No one was thinking of the general welfare. And this was to remain the dominant note of the first Duma. Muromzev, its chairman, although he was an intelligent man, sometimes ventured so far as to claim that the decisions of the Duma were infallible. Among the deputies were many men prominent for their mental and intellectual qualities, but they all made the same mistake of attacking the past and proposing laws which would have led to anarchy and which no Government would have accepted. The result was that the Duma was dissolved.

Goryemkin, Witte's successor as Minister of State, worn out, sent in his resignation, and was replaced by Stolypin. Shortly after the latter's accession to office, an attempt to take his life was made in his own villa. A motor car carrying alleged petitioners drew up in front of his house and, as he prepared to receive them, they hurled a bomb to the ground. Stolypin remained unhurt, as if by some miracle, but his daughter's legs were severely wounded.

After this catastrophe, Stolypin moved to the Winter Palace. The Emperor called on him, and when he heard about the dangerous condition of the Minister's daughter, he gave him the address of a "holy man," by whose prayers the young girl would be cured.

This was the first time that I had ever heard of Rasputin. I believe that at that time, the Emperor did not yet know him, but that the Archmandrit Theophan, Rector of the Ecclesiastical Academy, had told the Emperor a great deal about him. Shortly after this, the Metropolitan Antonin said to me, in regard to Rasputin: "If only Grisha does not work his way up to Their Majesties! He is a dangerous—a very crafty person, who could do much harm."

But Theophan had already introduced the miracle man to the Grand Duchess Militsa Nikolayevna, and she, in turn had brought him to the Empress.

By the Summer of 1907, the rumor was already current that the Tsarina was receiving the "staretz" (holy pilgrim) very secretly. He was usually brought to the small gate of the Alexander Palace opposite the Znamensk Church in the evening. From there he would walk through the garden to the Empress's balcony where he was received by those in her confidence, who conducted him to her by a spiral staircase. I do not know who else was present at those meetings, but I do know that the Tsar and Anna Vyrubova always participated in them.

CHAPTER XXI

The Tsarina Nervous Illness—Futile Battle of the Physicians Against Anya Vyrubova—Death of the Princess Galitzine —I Succeed Her—The Growing Influence of Rasputin—The Secret of the Imperial Family—Enmity Between Witte and Stolypin—A Conversation with Stolypin in the English Embassy. The Festivities at Kiev and Their Tragic End—I am the Tsaritsa's Guest in Livadia—The Unsociability of the Empress and Her Daughters.

WHEN I returned from a trip abroad in 1907, I found the Empress looking miserable. Although I knew that she did not like such inquiries, I asked her how she felt.

"Oh, I am so ill," she said. "I don't know why, but I am miserable."

This was the beginning of a malady which had its source in a severe nervous disorder. Anya never left the Empress at this time, sympathized with her, kissed her hands, and declared that no one except herself took the Tsarina's condition seriously enough, and that she alone felt any sympathy for the Empress's illness.

Doctor Fischer, the official physician, an intelligent and excellent man, had realized that the physical trouble of his patient was nothing more than a mild form of influenza, of no importance at all, but that her real malady lay in the nature of her nervous system, affected as it was by her mystic ecstasy. Finally the doctor decided to speak to the Vyrubova, appeal to her friendship for the Empress, and beg her to leave the Empress for some time. Only in this way, he said, would it be possible to remove the patient to a different type of moral, spiritual and physical atmosphere and thus cure her.

Anya's only answer to this proposal was a laugh, and Doctor Fischer realized that he could count on no help from that quarter. He therefore asked the Emperor for his dismissal, and resigned as Physician to Her Majesty.

He was replaced by a Doctor Eugeni Sergeyevich Botkin, whom Anya had recommended. She had called him in one evening by telephone, when she thought the Empress was dying. Consequently, the good Botkin owed his post to the Vyrubova, and for that reason alone he became her devoted friend.

The condition of the Empress, however, did not improve. Although her heart was organically sound, she suffered from its temporarily weakened condition, and lay on her couch constantly, even at luncheon. She would appear regularly for dinner, however, no matter how ill she might be, always *en grande toilette,* and wearing her marvelous jewels. Anya always dined with Their Majesties.

In the Autumn of 1908, I celebrated the twenty-fifth anniversary of my prison work, and was touched to the core at the manifestations of friendship and honor shown to me on that occasion. The Empress wrote me a very nice letter, and the Metropolitan Antonin volunteered to celebrate the Mass himself. My dear Princess Galitzine was still able to take part in this event. She died suddenly in the beginning of 1909.

After the funeral of my friend, I straightway went to Tsarskoye Selo, where the Empress asked me to call on her. After a brief conversation about our mutual loss, she said:

"And now, dear Madame Zizi, you will always remain with us and take over the post of the late princess."

When I drew her attention to my advanced age and told of my misgivings concerning the uncertain state of my health, whereby I might prove a burden to Her

Majesty, she would not listen to me. Rather, she promised not to tax my strength too much, and saw to it that I was appointed officially forthwith. Strictly speaking, nothing had been really changed in my life by means of this appointment, as I had lived in Tsarskoye Selo so often before, except that the large, beautiful apartment which had been Princess Galitzine's in the Winter Palace was now at my disposal. I gathered up some of my furniture and a few heirlooms and paintings that I had inherited from my parents, and after my return from the country I completed the furnishing of the handsome new apartment.

In the meantime Stolypin had grasped the reins of the Government firmly in his hands, imbued with the earnest desire to serve his Emperor and his country to the best of his ability. Under such circumstances, his time was naturally very precious, yet he came to my first reception in the Winter Palace. At that little dinner, I also entertained the German Ambassador, Count Pourtalès, his wife, and some other diplomats, and the Grand Duchesses Xenia and Olga Alexandrovna with their husbands, and the Greek Prince Christophe. Madame Plevitskaya sang some folk songs and was heartily applauded. The evening was informal and pleasant, and Stolypin congratulated me and told me how pleased he had been with the truly Russian atmosphere of my party.

The friendship between the Tsarina and Anya Vyrubova became closer than ever in those days, and the latter's influence increased in power while she herself was completely the creature of Rasputin. She constantly drove to his apartment in the Gorokhovaya and there received instructions from him as to how the Empress was to be guided. Anya actually regarded him as a saint, who uttered Heaven-inspired words, and she sincerely believed in his infallibility.

Who was this man, who had so great an influence not only over simple individuals but, one might say, on the course of the world's history? I can say nothing from my own impressions, as I never saw him and had always refused to make his acquaintance. It was only when the Empress particularly insisted upon it that I could be induced to speak on this subject, and gradually she realized that my aversion to Rasputin was not to be shaken. She, however, could not be convinced of anything that people might say against him, and declared repeatedly that it was the Devil who had suggested such ideas to them.

Now it was in vain that the Rector Theophan, who had originally introduced Rasputin to the Court, wrote to the Emperor full of contrition, and deplored his misfortune at having patronized so unworthy a man. For the consequence of Theophan's honest zeal was that he fell into disgrace and lost his post.

When the Governor of Moscow submitted a documentary report on the dissolute life Rasputin had led, he was removed from office, because by voicing an objection to the "holy man," he had incurred the Tsarina's hatred.

In vain, too, were the unflagging efforts of her former friends, Militsa and Stana Nikolayevna, to open the Tsarina's eyes about Rasputin. They resulted only in a violent scene of which they told me afterwards. It put an end to their once cordial friendship with the Empress.

Rasputin influenced the Empress mainly through his insistence on her guilt in regard to her son's illness. He claimed that the life and health of her child could be preserved only by the prayers of a God-sent saint. She told me that once when little Alexei was suffering a particularly serious attack, the physicians had insisted that the patient live permanently in the South, preferably in Egypt, as nothing would be so pernicious for his health as the damp, northern climate. In despair at this, the

Empress sent for Rasputin, who proclaimed with shining eyes:

"Fear not—your child need not leave you! Believe in the omnipotence of God, who has sent me to guard your son!"

In order to judge the Tsarina's actions fairly, one must realize that she literally trembled for the life of her child every minute of the time, for the slightest fall or blow might spell death for the little patient. This constant excitement was the actual cause of her serious nervous trouble, which was naturally increased by her desire to hide it from those surrounding her.

Not even in 1912, in Spala, when the child was battling for its life and suffering horrible pain, did the usual life of the monarchs change in its outward aspect. The dinners in company of their suite continued as before, the same meaningless conversations were held, and the Tsar went shooting as if nothing were happening. This manner of hiding every manifestation of emotion or excitement was also taught to the children. Accordingly, they never mentioned a word in regard to the family's relations with Rasputin. To be sure, the Tsarina's daughters sewed shirts for the "friend" and adored him, but it was kept a strict secret and it bound the participants still closer to one another, separating them still further from the rest of the world.

The young Grand Duchesses associated with no one, and generally behaved like young savages. Their social life expressed itself in childish flirtations with the officers of the "Standart" or with the convalescents in their hospitals. In all these activities their confidante was Anna—a fact well known to and evidently approved of by the Empress. Gradually everyone was judged by them according to his or her attitude toward Rasputin. Whoever praised him was "good." Whoever objected to him was "bad." Even Ministers of State were appointed on the basis of this criterion. One can imagine how thoroughly this situation was exploited by countless intriguers, business men and adventurers.

Stolypin was still at the helm and determined not to allow any interference with his regime. Accompanied by Krivoshine, the Secretary of Agriculture, he made tours of inspection all over Russia and Siberia, in order to convince himself of the actual conditions of the Empire. But Stolypin had many enemies, and among these, unfortunately, was Witte. The Count, still full of energy, talent and spirit, was convinced that he was better able to direct Russia's internal politics, and suffered deeply because of his impotence at a critical time like this. But in view of his unfriendly relations with the Emperor, he had no chance of becoming Prime Minister again.

Characteristic of this relationship was a conversation which the Princess Galitzine once had with the Emperor.

"It would be interesting to open a person's brain," she said, "and see what is hidden in it."

"Whose brain is it that seems so interesting to you?" asked the Tsar.

"The brain of Count Witte."

"That's very simple. You would merely find that he hates me as much as I hate him."

Witte had always been Stolypin's opponent, and his opposition became particularly evident when the question of introducing the Zemstvo (rural Assembly) in Poland arose. Witte intrigued to the utmost against it and tried to win the State Council to his side but the Emperor gave Stolypin his consent. The latter's triumph, however, endured but a short time. Vladimir Fyodorvich Trepov, who had the special privilege of calling on the Emperor at any time in case of important business, used this opportunity to submit a number of counter-arguments to the Tsar, whereupon the latter retracted his former decision. Stolypin replied by sending in his resignation.

It happened at that time that Buchanan, the English ambassador, was giving a dinner one night, and that Stolypin and his wife were among the guests. After dinner he sat down beside me, and when I expressed my regrets about the latest development, he said:

"I could not act otherwise—I knew well what I was doing. If the Tsar does not trust me, there remains nothing else but to go!"

"Isn't it possible to cancel your resignation?" I asked sympathetically.

"Only the Emperor can answer that." And he rose, said good-bye to his host, and left.

Surprising as it may seem, the whole conflict was settled in the end. But it had required the united efforts of all the Grand Dukes and the Empress-Mother, Maria Fyodorovna, who beset the Tsar and would not let him be until he had consented to ask Stolypin to withdraw his resignation. Peter Arkadievich Stolypin finally gave in, but only on the condition that Trepov's program be refused and his own carried out. The Emperor wisely complied with Stolypin's requests, but his self-love was acutely wounded. He never forgave Stolypin for his domination of the affair, and the symptoms of the perceptibly cooling friendship between the Tsar and Stolypin, naturally did not go unnoticed by the Prime Minister's antagonists. When we arrived in Kiev in August of 1911, I noticed by many small indications that Stolypin's political star was beginning to grow dim.

Festivities in Kiev kept us very busy. Many of the Polish ladies had come from their country estates, among them some of my relatives. The Nobility-Marshal himself was my nephew. He and his beautiful wife aided me in getting acquainted with all the guests. Accompanied by the wife of the Governor General, Trepov, I drove through the city constantly, visiting, in the name of the Empress, all the charitable institutions and home industry enterprises.

The conclusion of our sojourn in Kiev was to be celebrated by a performance at the big theatre, to which only holders of tickets marked with their names were to be admitted. The Place was crowded. The Polish aristocracy *en grande toilette,* the Emperor with his daughters and Prince Boris of Bulgaria in the stage box, I with the Ladies of Honor and two cavaliers in the adjoining box. All the Ministers of State sat in the front row of the parquet.

The curtain had dropped on the end of the first act, and the orchestra was playing an intermezzo, when suddenly there was a metallic sound which I believed had come from some defect in the curtain machinery. Stolypin, who had been standing directly in front of us at that moment, fell back in his seat, and was immediately surrounded by his colleagues. A wave of excitement rolled over the theatre, and I heard cries from every direction, and the rows of seats began to grow empty rapidly. By the time I realized what had happened, I was in the adjoining box. The Emperor was standing erect, but he was as pale as death. Tatyana Nikolayevna was weeping. In the meantime the Prime Minister, seriously wounded, had been carried out. The orchestra broke into the National Hymn, and the audience sang the words. The Emperor stepped to the front of his box—his face had not yet regained its color—and thanked the public. The murderer had been caught as he was trying to make his escape in the midst of the confusion.

One can imagine the mood in which we drove home. The Tsar and the children hurried to calm the Empress, while we remained on the porch and discussed the tragedy at length. Trubetskoy, who had served in the Japanese War, was of the opinion that Stolypin's chances were bad. Wounds of this nature, he said, were usually fatal. A weight of sadness lay on my heart.

Olga Borisovna Stolypin had been notified of the tragedy by telegraph, and a special train to Kiev had been provided for her. At first it seemed that all her hopes for her husband's recovery were justified, as the family had found the patient fully conscious, but his temperature soon rose, and late on the evening of September 5th he breathed his last.

The murderer—it was discovered—was a Jew who had some connections with the Okhrana. It was by this means that he had been able to effect an entrance into the theatre.

I stayed in Kiev until the first funeral Mass, and at the invitation of the Empress, I went from there to Livadia in the Crimea. There the magnificent new palace for the Imperial family had just been finished. The Empress herself had directed its construction from afar, and had chosen furniture and materials, so that everything was beautifully appointed.

Even at Sebastopol the blue sea and the bluer sky enchanted me. I was awaited by two motor cars, one of which carried my luggage. Then came a drive of three hours' duration, which increased my already boundless enthusiasm for the beauty of the landscape. As we reached the palace, all the dear Ladies of Honor rushed out to greet me affectionately. We were to occupy the newly built wing of the palace which had been divided into small but charming apartments. Each one of us had her own balcony, from which one had a marvelous view of the sea. Everything was new, elegant, clean and cozy.

While I was still in the tub, the Empress sent for me. I hurried as quickly as possible to thank Her Majesty

Tsar Nicolai II as Crown Prince

Tsar Nicolai and Tsarina Alexandra

Grand Duchess Maria Pavlovna in Old Russian Court Costume

for her kind attentions to me, and she received me in the most charming manner. Then we spoke of other things, and she begged me to talk to the Ladies of Honor and bring them to their senses. They had grown jealous of Anya, the Empress said, and had behaved arrogantly toward her. From the moment of my arrival I had had a dark premonition that all was not well, and sure enough, now it had become my task to re-establish domestic peace. I understood very well why the ladies were jealous of Anya Vyrubova, but I explained to them that as she was a guest here, we would have to make the best of it, and that we must try to behave decently to her. We did arrive at a sort of truce.

I did a good deal of driving about the environs of Yalta, never tiring of the beautiful scenery which met the eye in no matter what direction it turned, and I remember telling the Emperor how fortunate it was to have so enchanting a spot in our own Russia, and not to have to seek one abroad.

On November 3rd Olga Nikolayevna reached the age of sixteen, and was declared of age. A ball in her honor had been arranged at the Palace, and all the young people of the court, as well as the officers of the "Standart" and the Alexander Cavalry Regiment had been invited. I heartily enjoyed the merriment of the dear little Grand Duchesses, and secretly hoped that they might begin to like society and companions suitable to their distinguished position. In this, however, I was to be disappointed for, under their mother's influence, they remained averse to all festivities.

The Queen of Roumania said to me once:

"Things are different with us. In your country, the sovereigns are demigods, who may do anything they please. We have had to work to win the acknowledgment of our people, and I always teach my children:

'Everyone bears the duties of his position. Our duty is to earn the love of our subjects, to be amiable and agreeable.' The children know very well what they owe to society, and even my little one, who is only five, is polite and never forgets a greeting or a courtesy."

But our Empress paid no such deference to the opinion and criticism of those surrounding her, and it never occurred to her that their views, under certain conditions, might be of considerable importance.

CHAPTER XXII

Conversations with the Grand Duke of Hessia—The Empress Opens a Charity Bazaar—On the Battlefield of Borodino—The Romanov Jubilee—A Trip Along the Volga with the Imperial Family—Strange Manner of the Vyrubova—A Jewish Deputation to See the Tsar—The Roumanian Crown Prince Woos a Daughter of the Tsar — Their Majesties Visit Roumania—The King of Saxony in St. Petersburg—The War—The Empress-Mother Against Emperor William—The Empress Alexandra Becomes a War Nurse—The Grand Duke Nicolai Nikolayevich Falls Into Disgrace—A Domestic Council—"I Wear Trousers Under My Skirts"—Suspicious Rumors—High Treason—The Lonely Tsar—Deceptive Hopes.

We returned to the Crimea in the Spring of 1912, at the end of Lent, intending to spend Holy Week and Easter there. Our expectation of Spring weather in the South proved false at first, for we had snow even on Easter night. But it suddenly grew warm, and all at once the fruit trees began to bloom and the country looked more fairy-like than ever.

The Empress's brother, the Grand Duke of Hessia, had arrived in Livadia with his wife and his two boys. The Tsarina had always been more friendly with him than with her sisters, who were much older than herself, and throughout their childhood her brother had been her playmate. She had been looking forward to his visit with great impatience and pleasure, and he in turn gave every evidence that distance had not diminished his affection for his sister.

When I asked the Grand Duke how he had found his sister's looks and temper, he answered:

"My sister? She is splendid. Only you people here

don't know how to treat her. The Tsar is an angel, but he doesn't know how to deal with her. What she needs is a superior will which can dominate her, and which can, so to speak, bridle her."

Our talk then shifted to the Grand Duchess Elizabeth, his older sister, who had withdrawn to a convent after the murder of her husband.

"She was right," he commented. "For her life was broken, and she is building it up again according to her present need. Now that she has no other obligations to the world around her, she is dedicating herself to those religious experiences which will bring peace to her."

Toward the end of our stay in Livadia, the Empress arranged a charity bazaar. Countless articles, sewed or painted by the Tsarina and her daughters had been prepared for this purpose. The Bazaar was held at the Molo, and the imperial yacht, the "Standart," served as our lounging quarter and stock room. The Empress was in excellent humor, and sat behind her counter throughout the day, handing the articles to their purchasers herself. Naturally her counter was besieged by crowds who wanted something made by Her Majesty's own hands. The wave of warm sympathy and admiration which flowed toward her evidently did her good, and she was amiable and beautiful as I had never before seen her. Perhaps the fact that Anna was absent added to that favorable change.

The commemoration of the centenary of the battle against Napoleon was to be celebrated that Summer. Every historical spot of the great campaign was to be visited. In Borodino, Their Majesties went to see the local convent which had been founded by the widow of a nobleman who had fallen on the battlefield of Borodino. This lady, a Narishkin before her marriage, figures in an episode characteristic of Nicholas I.

It seems that, relying on the Emperor's repeatedly evidenced favor, she had asked him to pardon her brother, who was languishing in Siberia in consequence of his participation in the DeKabrist revolt. This plea seemed so monstrous to the Emperor that he rose brusquely and left the room. Not long after the incident, however, the Tsar invited her to view the Imperial Manoeuvres on the field of Borodina. She was to stand next to the Emperor, while the troops passed by, and was to receive all the gestures of military honor with him. According to the ideas of Nicholas I, such a distinction was great enough to compensate her for all her losses. And the Tsar was astonished beyond measure when, instead of being overcome by the beatitude of this privilege, the poor woman swooned at his side.

In February of 1913 the grand festivities in honor of the tri-centenary rule of the Romanovs were begun. A gala service was held in the Kasan Cathedral, attended by representatives of all the foreign powers and by the Patriarch of Antiochia, who acted as the Ambassador of the Eastern Church.

In the Spring we made an interesting trip, one which was to be a replica of the historical voyage of the first Romanov Tsar, Michail Fyodorovich, before his accession to the throne. In Vladimir we admired the splendid cathedral built by Andreas Bogolyubski in the Thirteenth Century. It was surprising to discover the degree of perfection which Russian art had attained even at that early period. In Nizhni-Novgorod we visited several nunneries, after which we boarded the steamer which brought us to Kostroma. There, the local populace received us with indescribable enthusiasm, and at our departure, whole droves of people threw themselves into the Volga, and swam alongside our boat as escorts.

Glowing with satisfaction, the Empress said to me at the sight of these devoted souls:

"Now you can see for yourself what cowards those State Ministers are. They are constantly frightening the Emperor with threats and forebodings of a revolution, and here—you see it yourself—we only need show ourselves, and at once their hearts are ours."

At Yaroslav we made another stop. The future Patriarch Tikhon delivered an address to the Emperor and then conducted us through the beautiful churches, decorated with paintings, which showed a distinct resemblance to Italian art. At a fair especially arranged for the Emperor the inhabitants of the Government displayed the products of their trades and industries. A brilliant soirée arranged by the nobility of that city concluded our visit to Yaroslav. After making another stop at Rostov, our historical voyage was completed, leaving us with many wonderful memories. Then back, by Moscow, to Tsarskoye Selo.

Once, while we were en route, I heard the Emperor say that the more interested he became in Russia's past, the deeper grew his love for his country. He added that in the future he intended to take a number of such trips along the Volga, to the Caucasus, and even as far as Siberia. What peaceful plans! Everything seemed so calm and secure in those days!

The Autumn found us in the Crimea again. This time Anya Vyrubova was with us but, as usual, I saw little of her. When she appeared at the Imperial table, one could not help noticing the shocking manner in which she tried to flirt with the Emperor. She always chose a place at table from which she could see him well, and she put no restraint on her eyes. Sometimes she would disappear for days, and then everyone knew that she had gone to Sebastopol to meet Rasputin.

The Empress never appeared at the official noontime meals, but always had her luncheon served on her balcony, usually eating alone or with one of her children. She would join the Court circle only after they had risen from luncheon and assembled on the white marble terrace. The guests formed into easy groups, which were usually augmented by the arrival of statesmen from St. Petersburg, or newly appointed high officials who had come to present themselves to the Tsar.

On one of these occasions I met Yanushkevich, the Director of the Military Academy, whom the Tsar had appointed Chief of the General Staff, on a sudden impulse. Speaking to me about this appointment one day, the Tsar said:

"Sometimes, as I face the task of selecting a man for a post, I am assailed by a positive certainty that a certain person is fitted for that place. And I have had the experience that this instinct is always right."

Yanushkevich, on the other hand, confided to me that his appointment had come to him out of a blue sky, and that he did not know how to justify the Tsar's great confidence in him. Subsequent events did indeed prove that Yanushkevich was not able—despite his good intentions—to master all the staggering tasks of this responsible position.

While we were in Livadia, a deputation of old Karaim—that Jewish tribe which is supposed to have emigrated from Palestine even before the Babylonian Captivity—called on the Emperor. The Tsar was very well impressed by the venerable men with their white beards, and he conversed with them at some length and animatedly. I, too, asked them many questions regarding their customs and traditions, and I got the impression that they were very much pleased by my interest in their history, which dates back thousands of years.

On November 3rd, the birthday of the Grand Duchess Olga was celebrated by a ball, just as it had been the year before. Shortly after this, I left for Moscow to see my brother who was ill. I stopped at the Kremlin, and spent the two weeks of my stay in Moscow chiefly in the company of the dear Princess Odagevski, the wife of the Palace Steward.

In the course of the following Winter, Prince Carol of Roumania arrived in St. Petersburg with the intention of asking for the hand of the Grand Duchess Olga. Sasonov, whose aim it was to divert Roumania from the Triple Alliance, considered him a fine candidate and hailed this union which fitted so well into his own plans. In fact, he expressly insisted upon it! As a member of the Hohenzollern family, the Roumanian Prince was on excellent terms with the German Imperial House; in addition he was a Greek Catholic, a fact which facilitated matters, and relieved the situation of what would have been an embarrassing difficulty.

When he visited me shortly after his arrival, he impressed me as a well-educated, well-bred and sympathetic young man. I asked him, incidentally, how it had happened that his father was a Catholic, while the Prussian Hohenzollerns were, without exception, Protestants. He explained that during the Reformation, the reigning branch had accepted the new doctrine, but that the other, the Roumanian line, had remained Catholic. King Carol had not changed his faith at the time of his accession to the throne, but had agreed to bring up his descendants in the Orthodox faith.

The Grand Duchess Olga had maintained a state of cold reserve in the face of this courtship, and it seemed to me that she was far from delighted at the thought of marriage to a Roumanian Prince. Nevertheless, it was agreed that the Tsar and his family would visit Konstanza from the Crimea in the following Spring.

This agreement was carried out, and incidentally gave me an opportunity of seeing the old Queen Elizabeth again, after an interval of fifty years. She was a highly educated and cultured lady, whose poems I had read in part, and rather admired.

The Roumanian Army was presented to the Emperor in a grand parade, and altogether the Bucharest Court did everything to make the Tsar's visit as splendid and impressive as possible. Among all the Roumanian statesmen, Bratianu attracted my particular attention, and I conversed at some length with him. After the parade and the subsequent dinner, the Royal family visited us on board the "Standart," and as we made our cordial farewells that evening, it was mutually agreed that our hosts would visit us the following Autumn in Yalta.

Soon after our visit to Konstanza, the centenary of the annexation of Bessarabia was to be celebrated at Kishinev. The unveiling of a monument erected for this purpose took place with the usual pomp. The most prominent personages of the city were received on the balcony of the Nobility Hall, on which occasion I tried to present as many people as possible to Their Majesties.

It was good to be back in Tsarskoye Selo, and to enjoy a few moments of rest, but only a short while later, the Centenary of the Battle of the Nations at Leipzig was commemorated, and the King of Saxony arrived in St. Petersburg for that purpose. He seemed a rough soldier, averse to court ceremonies. During one of the big dinners, the Emperor drank a toast to him, and it was then that he especially recalled the brotherhood-in-arms which existed between the German and Russian troops. None of us, seated at the festive board that night, could even remotely suspect that presently Germans and Russians would face each other as foes on the battlefield.

I had gone to the country in order to prepare there for the season at Livadia, when suddenly the report of the murder of the heir to the Austrian crown broke upon my peace. Being so far away from the capital, I was not very well able to follow its later political and diplomatic developments, and was therefore horrified when the papers published the fact that war had broken out.

I hurried back to St. Petersburg as quickly as I could, but the railway lines were already crammed with troops and army material, so that I could reach St. Petersburg only after many delays. I found the Empress about to go to her mother-in-law in Peterhof, and I heard from her own lips how impressive the Tsar's address to the people had been.

The next day, I too went to Peterhof, to see the Empress-Mother. She expressed herself about Germany in the most violent terms, and accused the Emperor William of having wantonly started the war. From Peterhof we went to Moscow where, according to an old tradition, the Tsar proclaimed the declaration of a war to the nation verbally. Vast crowds of humanity pressed through the Red Gate into the court of the Kremlin, acclaimed the Emperor and prayed on their knees for the victory of the Russian arms.

But blood had already been shed at the border, and our armies had to retreat before the Austrian onslaught, which broke through Galicia. The Grand Duke Nicolai Nikolayevich published a manifesto which announced the reëstablishment of the United Polish Kingdom, a measure which I considered right and proper.

From the beginning, the Empress had devoted herself to the nursing of the wounded with the greatest zeal and had organized military hospitals, ambulance trains, and divisions of Sisters of Charity. She and her two oldest daughters had taken the prescribed course for nurses, and had received their diplomas from the hand of the Chief Surgeon of Tsarskoye Selo. A hospital station for wounded officers was opened in one wing of the palace and operated under my management. There were, besides, several other provisionary hospitals in Tsarskoye Selo, and the Empress worked in all of them with the most admirable devotion.

Although her closest relatives—among them her own brother—were fighting on the German side, she regarded herself as absolutely Russian. It would be nothing but calumny to accuse her of sympathy with the enemy! She had distinct talent for organization, and in that first year of the World War she gave repeated proof of it. Among other things, she was responsible for the existence of the excellent Orthopedic Institute, headed by Dr. Wrede, which was the result of her own initiative to its minutest detail. The trained nurses' school for infants, which she had founded, constantly educated young girls for their vocation, and their activities served to reduce the death rate among babies.

Over against all these good qualities which the Tsarina displayed stood her stubborn insistence on her relationship with Rasputin. It seemed that these relations with the "Staretz" were concomitant with an actual mental derangement of a strange nature. I once spoke to Dr. Botkin about it, and he said sadly:

"I fully agree with you, and today I reproach myself for not having discovered the pathological character of the case long before this."

Nineteen-fifteen brought with it the chain of bitter disappointments which is well known. The war developed as unfavorably as possible for us, and one hope after another collapsed. Yet the Grand Duke Nikolai Nikolayevich continued to be popular, while the general dissatisfaction seemed to center upon the Ministry of War. Suchomlinov, the Secretary of War, was accused of being under the domination of his wife, who in turn was being influenced by some notorious business men. Thus an unwholesome, more than doubtful atmosphere enveloped the Ministry, and in addition there was the fact that Madame Suchomlinov belonged to the circle of Anna Vyrubova, and thus had access to the Empress.

The authority of the Grand Duke Nikolai Nikolayevich rested mainly on his manner of treating the soldiers correctly. Besides, he demanded as much coöperation from the officers as from the troops. This attitude was resented in some interested circles and used as a pretext for accusing him of treason. They informed the Tsar that the Generalissimo was nursing secret plans of usurping the throne and sending the Empress to a convent. Prince Orlov, Chief of the Imperial Privy Office, was also accused of complicity in this plan. The latter was a man of proved integrity who should have been above suspicion.

Acting on the advice of Rasputin, however, the Emperor finally decided to transfer the Grand Duke to the Caucasus and to take over the Chief Command of the Russian Army himself. When the Empress informed me of these events, I stubbornly refused to believe in the truth of the accusation against the Grand Duke, which would be that of High Treason. But she insisted that irrefutable proofs of it were in the Emperor's hands.

"And now," she cried, "that its fate lies in the hands of the Tsar, Russia is safe!"

As I stood there engrossed in thought, I happened to muse aloud that the Grand Duke was very popular. Whereupon she bridled, and retorted sharply:

"The Emperor is no less popular."

I realized that the task of taking command of the Army plus the general business of Government would prove too much for the Emperor's strength, and I had the conviction that this presumptuous gesture had been inspired in him from without. I saw that in the future, the Empress, who thus far had never interfered in matters of Government, would play a more active role from now on.

Before the Tsar left for General Headquarters, he summoned all the dignitaries of State to the palace to consult with them on numerous matters. The Empress had come to town too, and I had accompanied her. The council was in session for a very long time, and when the Emperor finally emerged from the conference room, followed by the Ministry, one look sufficed to note the dejection and discord of the Government. Krivoshine, the Minister of Agriculture, looked black as night. Some time later he told me that on that day he had clearly foreseen the inevitable, imminent breakdown of the Empire.

On our way back to Tsarskoye Selo, the Empress was visibly irritated. Her face had broken out in red blotches, and she pulled off her glove so abruptly that she tore it.

"All these men are cowards," she cried. "I believe I am the only man among them. I wear trousers under my skirts."

It was only a short time later that the signs of general confusion began to appear. The Ministers of the various Departments were changed in quick succession; increasingly alarming rumors regarding Rasputin's influence spread through the city, and when Protopopov was finally appointed Minister of State, it was generally claimed that he had bought this post from Rasputin for fifty thousand roubles. The first flare of indignation was directed against the Empress, who was quite justly accused of influencing her husband according to Rasputin's will.

Assertions to the effect that while the Emperor was calling special attention to his inviolate solidarity with the Allies, she was secretly in contact with the Germans and working with them toward a separate peace. The situation had grown so alarming that the King of England wrote to the Tsar suggesting that he send the Empress to Sandringham for a period of rest.

Our astonishment at this unusual offer was doubled, however, when the English Ambassador, Sir George Buchanan, declared categorically in the Emperor's face, that he had absolute proof of a conspiracy which aimed at making a separate peace, the trail of which led to the Empress. The Tsar had denied this accusation indignantly, and when the Ambassador added that the Empress was generally hated, the Tsar refuted this statement by pointing to numerous letters of gratitude and devotion which she had received from officers and soldiers.

I happened to know all about these letters, for the Empress handed most of them to me to answer. I recognized many of the signatures as belonging to people who I knew were members of the "National Russian League." Under such circumstances, these avowals of devotion had no value at all, and only served to mislead the Empress in regard to the feeling of the public at large.

At the time we were outraged by Buchanan's behavior, and believed that the Ambassador had allowed himself to be duped by meaningless rumors. But since then I have been informed that the Ambassador had based his intervention on the report of the English Intelligence Office, and that there was a modicum of truth in it. There actually was a plot which was operating toward the goal of a separate peace, with Rasputin as a mediator. Knowing quite well that the Tsar would never consent to be an accomplice to such treason, the conspirators used their efforts to bring about the Emperor's abdication, whereupon they expected to place the Regency in the hands of the Empress. Consciously or not, Anna Vyrubova was the center of this intrigue, for it was common knowledge that almost all the Ministers of the Government came to consult with her.

All personages who could have raised objections to such policies had gradually been removed from Court, and even the Grand Dukes were overridden on principle. One day at a dinner at Tsarskoye Selo, I was seated next to the Grand Duke Sergei Michailovich, and asked him whether he came to Tsarskoye Selo often.

"No," he answered. "Never."

"But, I'm surprised. . . ."

"So am I," he answered.

"But," I continued, "you used to be the Emperor's playmate, and you're now holding a high office. Don't you ever converse with His Majesty about your work or your plans?"

"No, never. I report to the Minister of War. That's all."

The Emperor had grown lonely indeed, especially as Count Fredericks, the Secretary to the Court, who had now become his sole daily companion, had grown feeble with age. Fredericks had told his son-in-law that peace would be concluded on May 1st; in fact, he had laid a bet on it. Rasputin himself had firmly declared that the war would terminate on December 28th, a remark which had added not a little to strengthening Prince Yussupov's decision to have the "Staretz" gotten out of the way. That some definite action had become necessary to prevent decisive events from happening was shown by the passionate zeal with which the Grand Duchess Elizabeth urged and encouraged her nephew Dimitri to commit the murder.

Rasputin's awful end was indeed a terrific blow to the Empress, but in accordance with her manner, she never betrayed her feelings to the outside world. Christmas came as usual; there were Christmas trees for the guard of honor and for the wounded in the hospitals; we, too, received small gifts from the Tsarina. There was a good deal of talk about the imminent concentration of all the military forces of the Entente, and about a plan for dealing a blow to the German army by means of a concentrated attack. We waited impatiently for the snow to melt, which would then enable our fighting forces to stage a final offensive. We had no doubt that this time we would succeed in downing the opponent, for the German army was worn out and weak, and their supplies were growing insufficient, while our side was well supplied with food and weapons. Thus 1917 began with high hopes, which were cruelly shattered all too soon by the outbreak of the Revolution.

The Crown Prince in Livadia

Grand Duchesses Olga and Tatyana in Livadia in the uniform of their Regiments

CHAPTER XXIII

The Outbreak of the Revolution—No News of the Tsar—Arrival of the Captive Tsar—The Imperial Children Are Ill—Intrigues of Anna Vyrubova — Conversation with Their Majesties—My Conversation With Kerenski—The Emperor's Kiss of Peace—Kerenski Cross-Examines the Empress—The Imperial Family Spends Its Time in Mutual Instruction—A Heart-breaking Farewell—The Tsarina's Last Letter.

On February 23, 1917, I went to St. Petersburg for a few days. I had hardly arrived when the little Tsaryevich fell ill with the measles and in rapid sequence his two older sisters as well as Madame Vyrubova did likewise. I had intended to return to Tsarskoye Selo at once, but that same night I suffered a violent heart attack which was repeated several times. This malady, coming as it did after all the excitement of the past months, kept me captive in the Winter Palace.

Disturbances in the streets began to make their daily appearance; the people wanted bread, and working men roamed through the city without occupations since there was no more raw material on hand.

I shall now quote from my diary which I kept faithfully, even through the most horrible happenings.

February 27, 1917: Dr. Varevka came, beside himself: street-brawls, bombs, shootings and numerous wounded and dead. He was able to make his way to me only under great difficulties. Now the people are demanding not only bread but also a change of Government. It is not too late yet; the Emperor has not entirely lost his prestige; only Protopopov need be dismissed and a Ministry appointed which holds the confidence of the people. But the stubbornness of the Empress opposes any such concession, thanks to the satanic influence by which she is governed.

Events develop with maddening rapidity. Rodsyanko is at the head of a committee for the maintenance of order, one regiment after another joins him; all troops have gone over to the Duma. Two telegrams addressed to the Emperor have remained unanswered to this day. There are no more Cabinet Ministers—they all have resigned. There is a rumor that the house of the Secretary to the Court has been burned down. The sentry in front of the Palace has disappeared. A deputation is supposed to have left for Tsarskoye Selo to report to the Empress regarding the change of Government.

March 1. . . . No news of the Emperor; we don't know where he is. Someone has broken into the Empress's apartment at night. The guard has deserted her; the Imperial children are ill, the little fellow's temperature is 104. I know I ought to go to Tsarskoye Selo, but it is impossible to get there. There are no horses, no autos. . . . I telephone to Vladimir Volkonski, who advises me to wait. . . .

March 3rd: As always, the party representing order and moderation has been pushed aside by the Revolutionists and demagogues. They want a Republic, they want anarchy! Violence in the streets, many dead, houses are being looted. Büvting has been killed in the Tver, also one of the Vyazemskis. The Emperor has signed the document of abdication for himself and his son. . . . Despair. . . .

March 4th: Protopopov has capitulated. It is said that he has made ugly depositions regarding the Empress. The scoundrel! The fine wretch of an aide-de-camp, Sablin, was the first of the guard to swing over to the revolutionary side. Poor old Goryemkin arrested, carted away on a truck—sick!

March 5th: I have telephoned the Grand Duke Nicolai Nikolayevich to beg him to arrange for my going to Tsarskoye Selo. His answer was: "Wait a few days. At present there is danger. I shall keep you informed." Today things seem to look brighter. The new Government Ministers have taken their offices. Only the rabble, not satisfied with the Emperor's abdication, is talking of murdering him.

March 6th: An attack on Kerenski's life. Rodsyanko is threatened. The same story as that of the Girondists and Terrorists. Benkendorff telephoned me today that my apartment in the Alexander Palace was ready. I shall move there tomorrow. On Friday, the victims of the Revolution are to be buried on the Palace Square. My departure for Tsarskoye Selo with Lilly Obolenski. What heart-rending moments! Have seen the Empress. She is very gentle, very calm, and shows amazing magnanimity. She says that God is stronger than man. And she said it seemed that everything was beginning to smooth out, again! She doesn't even know that all that has happened has largely been her fault. We lunched with Benkendorff, and spent the afternoon with Buxhoeveden. The children are still very ill; the Grand Duchess Maria also developed measles today.

March 8th: Have been at Church to hear Mass. The deacon has been arrested. When he began to pray for the Tsar, the congregation started to hiss. Unspeakably sad! Have seen a few people crying from sympathy. Returned and am told by Benkendorff that we are arrested. We may not go out, or telephone; we may only write by way of the Central Committee. The Empress asked to have prayers said for the Emperor's trip. Refused!

March 10th: The Emperor's arrival today. I went downstairs to see him and remained standing behind the butler. He seems calm. Vanya Dolgoruki read us the document of the abdication. Fredericks, Nilov, Voyaikov are arrested. We discover that the garden gate through which the Emperor usually enters is locked. We look for the officer of the Guard, who claims to have mislaid the key. The Emperor waits a generous fifteen minutes, then says to Vanya: "I see we have to make haste to get away from here." Later he took a stroll in the small garden with Vanya. Officers dogged every one of his footsteps and called him "Colonel."

The Empress has asked me to come to tea at five o'clock. As an illustration of the incredible rapidity with which such catastrophes develop, I described the beginning of the Revolution of 1848 in Paris, to the Tsar. While we were still conversing, the Emperor was called away. An automobile with an officer of the Revolutionary Party had arrived. They wanted to see the Emperor, in person, for there was some doubt as to his actual arrest. After a little while, he returned and we resumed our friendly chat. What self-control! During some moments, while the Empress had left the room, he said to me: "Isn't she brave?" In the evening we all met at Benkendorffs' where we gathered, unspeakably depressed.

March 11th: Apraxin can stand it no longer and is leaving tomorrow. He went to say good-bye to the Empress, and told her she would have to part with Anna Vyrubova. The Empress was angry and stubborn.

March 13th: Things are growing worse. The Revolutionary Party does not want to let the Emperor go, for fear of intrigues, treason and betrayal of secrets. The Germans are making superhuman efforts to penetrate our Fronts. If they succeed, the way to St. Petersburg lies open before them. The delegate of the Provisional Government, Kotzebue, has come to see me, bringing news of

Maneuver near the Convent St. Sava

Maneuver near the Convent St. Sava

my family, from whom I had not heard in a long while, and also tells me that my beautiful cows in Stepanovski have been stolen. I am having a letter written to Silin, to get details. . . . Sad! Sad!

March 16th: It is a week today that we have been arrested. The little Grand Duchess Maria is very ill. An attack of pleurisy has developed in addition to the measles. Her temperature is 105. In Stepanovski, disorder, as everywhere; no police, no district chief, no guard. In case of an attack, I shall not defend it by arms—no hate, no bloodshed in that place where all my life I have tried to sow the seeds of loving-kindness. I feel weak these days. I have congestions in the heart and head when I think of the horror of violent death at the hands of a soldier. I believe it is soldiers who run along our corridors at night and rattle our doors, which we lock carefully from the inside. An evil sensation!

March 17th: Have gone out for the first time to get some fresh air. Taking advantage of the lovely sunny weather, I walked up and down the Terrace with Mary Benkendorff. The young Grand Duchesses are in the snowed-in Garden with the officers of the Guard. Anna Vyrubova is trying to attract Kotzebue and win him over to her interests. I doubt that he will fall a victim to her lies, for he is wise and crafty.

March 19th: Everybody is very sad. All the telegrams which the Empress has sent to the Tsar during the last weeks have been made public. The Empress is indignant, and I believe—scared. The antagonistic spirit toward her is increasing. It would be horrible if it ended in condemnation. I had been wishing ardently that they might let her go away.

March 20th: We have lost Kotzebue. Anna Vyrubova has sent for him and gotten him under her influence. The Empress also listens to her counsel. I believe that she has brought about everything systematically, and that her power over the Tsar was as great as that over the Empress. The whole situation is subtly permeated with occultism, mysticism and satanic suggestions! A compromise with the Vyrubova is impossible. We all ignore her completely, but Their Majesties spend every evening with her, and only come to us occasionally to chat about some indifferent matters. I regret Rasputin's murder; it was a sad and low act. The Revolution could not have been prevented for all that, and it would have broken out in consequence of Protopopov's regime alone.

March 21st: I am just looking out of the window and watch the Emperor as he takes his walk. He is in front, behind him Vanya, then the officer on duty. I feel a bitter ache. How far has he sunk who once owned the riches of the earth and a devoted people! How splendid his reign could have been, if he had only understood the needs of the era! Great news! Kerenski, the new Minister of Justice, and the new Commandant have just arrived with a large retinue, to inspect us and to take the Vyrubova away with them. The Empress is in despair.

March 24th: I have been with the Empress. We spoke of the imminent departure, and about the choice of persons to accompany Anna. She is angry with the young Grand Duchesses, because they did not go to see her while she had the measles. I said: "It is because they know that she has done evil things to you." She grew angry and cried: "Anna has devoted her whole life to me; it is wicked of you to say such things about her. I can never forgive you."

March 25th: A touching, uplifting and infinitely sad Mass. The priest comes only to perform his office; he speaks to no one. Only at the conclusion does he hold out the crucifix to be kissed, and delivers a short address into which he weaves a few consoling words. The Commandant and his people are present throughout the service and keep a strict eye on him. I went to the Empress and advised her in consideration of the approaching holy days, to forget her anger at the Court ladies, who had always given proof of their devotion. I was touched when she said to me: "The Emperor was forced to abdicate for the good of the country. If he had refused, a Civil War would have been the result. The chief thing is Russia's welfare. If this can be attained without us—the better!" The Commandant came to see me later. I liked him. He seems to be a man who desires what is good. He is a Republican, believes in the future magnitude of the movement, and is enthusiastic over the idea of liberty won by battle.

March 27th: A day of stirring events. Mary comes to tell me that ditches are being dug in front of the Alexander Palace to bury the victims of the Revolution. The Commandant appears after the services, and informs me that Kerenski, the Minister of Justice, is awaiting me in the Emperor's recption room. Kerenski tells me that it is absolutely necessary to separate the Tsar from his wife, and adds: "As the children are more attached to the father than to the mother, I believe we ought to leave them with the Emperor." I noticed that the man too was under the influence of those calumnies which pictured the Empress as a bad mother, and I said to him: "It would mean death to her. One can't imagine a more tender mother than she is. When the children are ill—and they are ill now—the Empress stays with them day and night. Her children are her life." After this, Kerenski asked some questions regarding her private life, and finally said: "If that's the case, we must leave the children to the mother. In any event it has become necessary, after a new discovery we have made from Madame Vyrubova's papers, to separate the couple." That stupid woman had evidently been very careless while under the domination of the rogues who had led her on.

March 28th: The papers found on Anna Vyrubova are said to be very compromising as they refer to espionage and a separate peace. If that is proved to be true, it would mean high treason and call for the utmost punishment. We know now that a plot of this nature really was afoot, and that the guilty participation of the Empress in trying to secure a separate peace, thus committing treason against Russia, has been definitely proved. I went to see the Empress in the evening. She was indignant at Kerenski's orders, and talked senselessly all night. She cannot understand anything, and has been screaming for an hour until she is hoarse. Very tiring.

March 29th: I am afraid that the diatribes of the Empress may reach the ears of the Government, which after all is trying its best to help the Tsar's family. I wish they understood what I realized a long time ago—that the Empress is a pathological case! This is her only excuse, and may become her only salvation.

March 30th: Botkin agrees with me entirely in regard to the Empress. He is one of the most decent people I know, and utterly devoted to the Tsar. The Empress is so unhappy that one must forgive her everything. She begged me to pray for Anna Vyrubova, which I promised to do. Before she went to confession, she sent me a cordial note: "My heart is so full, I have no words—" At Mass, she looked beautiful, sad, and immensely composed.

April 2nd: Easter! Grand, beautiful day, despite all human misery. Midnight Mass and morning reception in Their Majesties' apartments. The Emperor gave the prison guards the kiss of peace, and they were touched. Today at noon, congratulations and distribution of Easter eggs. The Emperor gave me one with his signature and said: Guard it well. It is the last—" The future is uncertain. Everything depends on the relative permanence of the Provisional Government or the superior power of the anarchists—danger is imminent!

April 20th: Sadness and silence. We are reading Chekhov at night. Nastinka, Isa and Vanya are dying of laughter. Mary Benkendorff is asleep. I find Chekhov a great talent, but it is counterbalanced by his vulgarity and abominable lack of any idealism.

April 26th: Kerenski is said to be coming here in order to cross-examine the Empress. I have been called in as witness to the conversation. I found her excited and in an irritated, nervous mood. She was prepared to say a number of silly things to him, but I succeeded in calming her, by telling her: "For the love of God, Your Majesty, don't say a word of all this. Remember that you are in his power and that you are risking the lives of your husband and children. Kerenski is trying his utmost to save you from the Anarchist Party. By interceding for you he is risking his own popularity. He is your only prop. Please try to understand the situation as it is. You are facing the greatest danger—don't spoil everything by a mistake."

At this moment, Kerenski entered, followed by the Commandant. He begged me to withdraw and remained alone with the Empress. I stepped into the small salon with the Commandant, and here we found Benkendorff and Vanya. A few minutes later the Emperor, returning from a walk, joined us there too. I stepped into a bedroom with him, and told him what was going on. Then we joined the Empress while Kerenski withdrew into the Tsar's study.

The Empress has been pleasantly impressed by Kerenski—she finds him sympathetic and honest. . . . One could arrive at an understanding with him, she thinks. I am hoping that he has received as favorable an impression of her. Kerenski was compelled to come again late at night, as a Revolutionary deputation from the Front had arrived in Tsarskoye Selo in order to see for themselves that the captives were secluded securely enough and to demand their transfer to the fortress. Kerenski was compelled to send for the Commandant in the middle of the night. It was a dangerous moment, but the forenoon's conversation had evidently left Kerenski with a good impression and everything remains as it has been. But Kerenski comes out victorious with only the greatest difficulty. As long as he is with us, we are more or less safe, but there will be no trip for us.

April 17th: The little Tsaryevich said to me the other day: "Papa has examined us. He was very much dissatisfied and said, 'Is that all you have learned?'" The daughters have volunteered to teach him and the parents are following their example. The Emperor has chosen History and Geography, the Empress Religion and German for their subjects. Isa is teaching English, Nastenka, History of Art and Music. All this is very good, for it keeps them busy and throws a ray of culture into this democratic home. This has impressed even one of the subalterns who takes turns in guarding the Emperor. He thinks that the Imperial Family has only lost its pedestal, and that the Emperor is gradually getting used to his present mode of life if he only is allowed the privilege of his habits, his walk, his five o'clock tea and the other meals!

April 27th: Have lunched with Their Majesties. The Empress is sad and silent; the children, happy. Have talked with the Tsar about History, the past, and about literature. He discovers advantages in his present position in that it gives him time to read. So far his only literature had consisted of State documents which dried up his mind.

May 2nd: Horrible changes! All the Generals are gone. No one can master this unbridled, dispersing Army. The soldiers are fleeing and deserting. The Government sits in council day and night. Kerenski has cried out in agony: "I regret that I did not die two months ago—I would have passed away with the illusion of my country's liberty. Are you citizens, or are you slaves who revolt?"

May 6th: The Emperor's Jour de Fete (Saint's day). Oh, what a sad day—ill—dreadfully cold—my salon is an ice house.

May 8th: Seriously ill in consequence of the terrible cold. No wood—I fear another attack of pneumonia and death, away from those I love. Also the trouble my death would cause Their Majesties. It seems to me that my presence is not important to the Empress now that I have put her in contact with Kerenski. He will protect her even without me.

When the Empress and Tatyana called on me, I expressed the wish to be transported to the big Palace. She said: "Why? Can't we all stay here together?" I told her that my illness would only cause her embarrassment and complications might result. Then I wrote to Kerenski asking him to make it possible for me to be installed in one of the lovely salons in the big Palace. He has consented.

When the Emperor heard that I was leaving, he called on me with Tatyana and Alexei, and after the children had gone he stayed with me for a long while. He was much moved, and I was no less so. I believe that both of us had a premonition that we would never be together again. We embraced repeatedly, and he kissed my hands incessantly. Later, the Empress came in and stayed two hours with me. I was very tired, she very affectionate, and still full of hopes for the success of the counter-revolution. She does not realize that any overthrow of the present power would only increase the danger of her position. But the illusion soothes her and helps her to bear present conditions.

On the next morning, she came again at ten o'clock and thanked me lovingly for having always been, so she said, a great help to her. She cried bitterly as she embraced me. Then the hospital attendants appeared with the stretcher. All had assembled in the salon to bid me farewell, the Empress and the children also. A few minutes later, I was in the big Palace and free!

I am now receiving frequent news bulletins from the Alexander Palace. The Emperor who had been breaking ice and shoveling snow during the winter, is cultivating a small vegetable garden on the front lawn of the palace, in order to do some physical work. All his co-captives share zealously in this labor, at which they spend the three hours allotted to them daily for their walk—from two to five in the afternoon. The Emperor enjoys this physical exertion.

July 18th: Kerenski has told the Emperor some time ago, that they could not remain in Tsarskoye Selo. Places of exile were mentioned and they agreed upon the Crimea. This suited the Emperor very well, and the packing of trunks began. Suddenly word came that all fur garments and whatever warm clothing there was, was to be taken along. Evidently it is not to be a trip to the Crimea but to the North. The cook who is to accompany the Imperial Family has received orders to prepare a five days' supply of food, and the Emperor has figured out that a five-day trip could only have Siberia for its goal.

The Tsar and the Grand Duchess Tatyana and Maria in Livadia

The Hospital in Tsarskoye Selo in the year 1915

The departure was settled for midnight. All were prepared to go; the boxes were packed and ready for transport. They waited thus all night, until five o'clock in the morning. Kerenski appeared from time to time, pushed everyone aside and spoke to them in arrogant tones in the presence of the Bolsheviki. But when the latter were gone, he behaved very correctly, even addressing the Tsar by his title.

The Grand Duke Michael, who had learned of the imminent departure only by accident, hurried over from Gachina at once, and begged Kerenski for permission to bid his brother farewell. Kerenski conducted him to the Emperor, who was completely surprised, sat down in a corner, and covering his ears with his hands told them: "You may talk at your pleasure." The Emperor was visibly moved and, as is often the case in moments of great stress and surprise, they had nothing to say to each other. As a matter of fact, this reunion only lasted a few minutes.

Shortly afterward, Kerenski stepped into the Emperor's study and said: "Your Majesty, have you confidence in me?" The Tsar hesitated, then looked at Kerenski and answered: "Yes."

"Very well, Your Majesty, do you believe that whatever I am doing is done to save you and not to ruin you? Do you believe it?"

The Emperor said: "I believe you."

Behind the iron fence of the Palace stood an immense crowd of people hooting and shouting menacingly. It would have been impossible to transport the Imperial Family through the main gate, so the motor cars were driven through the park to the Alexandrovsk Station. There the train stood ready for them. The Empress was pulled up with great difficulty and at once fell forward on her hands and knees.

On the previous evening, I had written a short note to the Empress anent the birthday of the Tsaryevich. I told her that I had recovered and was ready to return to her if I could be of any service. Her answer was the following letter:

"DEAR MADAME ZIZI:

"I embrace you with all my love for your kind words, prayer and wishes for our beloved ray of sunshine. We have the great consolation of praying before the shrine of the Holy Virgin of Znamenskoye at 2:30, and I shall remember you lovingly in my prayers, beloved friend. Thank you for all the things you said to me; how gladly would I press you to my heart, but that is impossible. You will understand how difficult it is for me, but we can do nothing; everything is in the hands of God, and I trust that we may see each other again. Forgive me for writing so short a note, but my heart is too full! God bless you! I beg you most urgently to write to me from time to time. We all embrace you and thank you for your love and friendship. May the Saviour keep you!

"Always yours with all, all my loving heart,

"A."

On the following day, came their departure, and I received one more note:

"DEAREST MADAME ZIZI:

"A word of tenderest farewell and blessing. I am grieved at leaving you without saying good-bye. My cordial thanks for the twenty-three years of your faithful love and friendship! You don't know how dear you are to me and to all of us. God bless you and keep you and spare you all sorrow! May He grant us the joy of another reunion in this life. Let me hear from you in the meantime. Farewell, my dearest, my maternal friend. My heart is too full to write any more.

"A."

THE END.